D1261319

The Moral Conditions of Economic Efficiency

In the late eighteenth century, Adam Smith significantly shaped the modern world by claiming that when people individually pursue their own interests, they are together led toward achieving the common good. But can a population of selfish people achieve the economic common good in the absence of moral constraints on their behavior? If not, then what are the moral conditions of market interaction that lead to economically efficient outcomes of trade? Answers to these questions profoundly affect basic concepts and principles of economic theory, legal theory, moral philosophy, political theory, and even judicial decisions at the appellate level.

Walter J. Schultz illustrates the deficiencies of theories that purport to show that markets alone can provide the basis for efficiency. He argues that markets are not moral-free zones and that achieving the economic common good does indeed require morality. He demonstrates that efficient outcomes of market interaction cannot be achieved without moral normative constraints and then goes on to specify a set of normative conditions that make these positive outcomes possible.

The Moral Conditions of Economic Efficiency does not depend on a particular ethical theory or on the overcited shortcomings of private property economies. Rather, it focuses on the process of market interaction itself to prove that selfishness alone cannot provide for the economic good.

Walter J. Schultz is a Professor of Philosophy at Cedarville University in Cedarville, Ohio.

Cambridge Studies in Philosophy and Law

GENERAL EDITOR: Gerald Postema
(University of North Carolina, Chapel Hill)

ADVISORY BOARD
Jules Coleman (Yale Law School)
Antony Duff (University of Stirling)
David Lyons (Boston University)
Neil MacCormick (University of Edinburgh)
Stephen Munzer (U.C.L.A. Law School)
Philip Pettit (Australian National University)
Joseph Raz (University of Oxford)
Jeremy Waldron (Columbia Law School)

Other Books in the Series:

Jeffrie G. Murphy and Jean Hampton: *Forgiveness and Mercy*
Stephen R. Munzer: *A Theory of Property*
R. G. Frey and Christopher W. Morris (eds.): *Liability and Responsibility: Essays in Law and Morals*
Robert F. Schopp: *Automatism, Insanity, and the Psychology of Criminal Responsibility*
Steven J. Burton: *Judging in Good Faith*
Jules Coleman: *Risks and Wrongs*
Suzanne Uniacke: *Permissible Killing: The Self-Defence Justification of Homicide*
Jules Coleman and Allen Buchanan (eds.): *In Harm's Way: Essays in Honor of Joel Feinberg*
Warren F. Schwartz (ed.): *Justice in Immigration*
John Fischer and Mark Ravizza: *Responsibility and Control*
R. A. Duff (ed.): *Philosophy and the Criminal Law*
Larry Alexander (ed.): *Constitutionalism*
Robert F. Schopp: *Justification Defenses and Just Convictions*
Anthony Sebok: *Legal Positivism in American Jurisprudence*
William A. Edmundson: *Three Anarchial Fallacies: An Essay on Political Authority*
Arthur Ripstein: *Equality, Responsibility, and the Law*
Heidi M. Hurd: *Moral Combat*
Steven J. Burton (ed.): The Path of the Law *and Its Influence*
Jody S. Kraus and Steven D. Walt (ed.): *The Jurisprudential Foundations of Corporate and Commercial Law*
Christopher Kutz: *Complicity*

The Moral Conditions of
Economic Efficiency

Walter J. Schultz

Cedarville University

CAMBRIDGE
UNIVERSITY PRESS

PUBLISHED BY THE PRESS SYNDICATE OF THE UNIVERSITY OF CAMBRIDGE
The Pitt Building, Trumpington Street, Cambridge, United Kingdom

CAMBRIDGE UNIVERSITY PRESS
The Edinburgh Building, Cambridge CB2 2RU, UK
40 West 20th Street, New York, NY 10011-4211, USA
10 Stamford Road, Oakleigh, VIC 3166, Australia
Ruiz de Alarcón 13, 28014 Madrid, Spain
Dock House, The Waterfront, Cape Town 8001, South Africa

http://www.cambridge.org

First published 2001

Printed in the United States of America

Typeface Times New Roman 10/12 pt.   *System* QuarkXPress [AG]

A catalog record for this book is available from the British Library.

Library of Congress Cataloging in Publication Data

Schultz, Walter J., 1950–
  The moral conditions of economic efficiency / Walter J. Schultz.
    p. cm. – (Cambridge studies in philosophy and law)
  Includes bibliographical references and index.
  ISBN 0-521-80178-8
  1. Economics – Moral and ethical aspects.   I. Title.   II. Series.
HB72.S348 2001
330–dc21
JK   00-052926

ISBN 0 521 80178 8 hardback

To my dear spouse, soul mate for life, and best friend,
Mary

Contents

Preface and Acknowledgments

I hope that this book contributes to a better understanding of the interconnection between morality and economic behavior. It is intended for those whose interests lie in legal theory, economic theory, moral philosophy, and political theory and for those who are concerned with ascertaining a moral basis for pluralistic, private property democracies. I also hope that the theoretical results of this work will prove useful to policy analysts, judges, legislators, and those involved in developing constitutions for emerging democracies.

Several perplexities, hunches, and heuristically fruitful concepts served to focus my interest in the moral conditions of economic efficiency. I first became interested in this issue while reading Adam Smith's *Wealth of Nations* and *Theory of Moral Sentiments*. It seemed to me then that there was a closer connection between morality and market behavior in Smith's writings than was made explicit. I am sympathetic to and inspired by what I believe is the intent of Jules Coleman's *Risks and Wrongs* and of David Gauthier's *Morals by Agreement*. A pluralistic democracy having a private property economy needs some common morality that respects a pluralism of moral traditions, is capable of guiding the common life of all, and underwrites its legal system. But, at the time, the relationship between morality and markets seemed to need greater clarification before competing traditions could come to any "agreement" or "rational choice contract." Since an overarching issue is social behavior, it seemed that some account of social behavior must be thrown into the mix as well. I found myself intrigued by Ludwig Wittgenstein's notion of a social practice but enlightened by Ronald Koshoshek's views of the same.

Musing over these perplexities, hunches, and concepts led to a closer examination of the presuppositions of the First Fundamental Theorem of Welfare Economics (or First Welfare Theorem), which is a precise version of Adam Smith's invisible hand. Simplifying assumptions cannot be avoided in social science. But sometimes it pays to reexamine those assumptions to see whether they can be expanded to cover other contributing factors. The more I considered the assumptions of the First Welfare Theorem and what they were supposed to accomplish, especially in view of Smith's moral theorizing and pre-Enlightenment views of property, the more I was drawn by the intuition that morality made economic efficiency possible for autonomous people.

I am grateful for the help I have received from several individuals. From Ronald Koshoshek I acquired the background framework of concepts for understanding social behavior that informed this project. Furthermore, his expert and forthright advice was instrumental in my being interested in moral rights and their relationship to economic analysis in the first place.

I am indebted to Daniel Johnson and William Thedinga for our weekly colloquium and for detailed written comments on several entire drafts. This work involves concepts and jargon germane to moral philosophy, economics, and law. There is always a risk of misunderstanding and misrepresentation when one adopts the specialized language of each these fields while addressing oneself to a problem common to all. Their sensitivity to the nuances of those languages and wonderful facility with correct English doubtlessly contributed greatly to the clarity of the finished project and to the accessibility of its ideas to non-experts. Any conceptual errors or stylistic oddities that occur in the manuscript are there because I ignored their advice.

For the uncompromising precision and thoroughness that Norman Dahl and Leonid Hurwicz showed in commenting on earlier drafts; for the intellectual stimulation and multidisciplinary expertise of Norman Bowie; and for the editorial comments, suggestions, and enthusiastic support of Peg Brewington, I am deeply grateful.

A Cedarville University Faculty Research Stipend enabled me to dedicate several months solely to this project.

But more than any, I thank my dear spouse and best friend, Mary, who in the operation of her business has always observed the moral normative constraints discussed herein, who has supported this project in countless ways, and who is happier than I am to see it finished.

The Moral Conditions of Economic Efficiency

1

Introduction and Synopsis

This work is a rigorous analysis of the moral conditions of economic efficiency and these two central questions focus its argument:

Question 1. *Can a population of strict rational egoists achieve efficient allocations of commodities through market interaction in the absence of moral normative constraints?*

If not, then we must ask:

Question 2. *What are the moral normative constraints and other types of normative conditions of market interaction leading to efficient outcomes?*[1]

Adam Smith's so-called Invisible Hand Claim has been subject to two centuries of theorization that has intensified in the last two decades. Yet in this time we have not achieved any consensus on the possible moral conditions of economic efficiency. My analysis provides a way to frame the issues rigorously and to answer the two central questions.

The first question defines my first task: to determine whether economically efficient outcomes of market interaction require moral (in contradistinction to legal) normative constraints; that is, whether the constraints needed for efficiency are normative, moral, and rational. I will demonstrate that efficient outcomes of market interaction cannot be achieved without a system of moral normative constraints for securing competitive behavior and a set of conventions for facilitating exchange, for coordinating supply and demand, and for internalizing certain types of externalities. After this is established, the second question defines my second goal: to specify a set of normative conditions that make efficient outcomes of trade possible.

Answers to these central questions affect not only basic concepts in economic theory but also fields for which economic analysis is important, including legal theory, moral philosophy, political theory, and policy analysis.[2] The concepts – market, perfect competition, perfectly competitive market, externality, and the First Fundamental Theorem of Welfare Economics – are all affected by answers to these questions. Both moral philosophy and political theory gain by taking the concepts and techniques of economic analysis into consideration. Appeals court judges and policy analysts often use economic efficiency as a factor in their decisions and proposals. Since, as I will show, economic efficiency requires moral normative constraints, such decisions and proposals must not undercut the moral conditions of economic efficiency.

This analysis requires clarifying some central concepts and making appropriate distinctions where necessary. There are two types of normative conditions of efficiency: normative constraints and conventions. In general, a normative constraint is a limit on an agent's range of possible actions and is constituted by a behavioral rule and a sufficient incentive to comply. Normative constraints can be either proscriptive or prescriptive. I will say more about normative constraint in the next section by contrasting it with morality. A *convention,* on the other hand, could be described as a coordinating rule. A regularity in social behavior emerges when each individual observes a convention by virtue of an incentive given by instrumental (or practical) rationality alone. For example, the conventions of grammar guide the use of a common language and enable communication. Communication would fail without such conventions. Economically efficient outcomes of trade require both normative constraints and conventions.

I specify a set of normative conditions, which I demonstrate to be not only necessary but also sufficient in theory for efficient outcomes of trade. These normative conditions are moral in nature. And I will show that moral norms or rules alone are not sufficient. Some type of enforcement is also necessary. I show that the only such mechanism is an internal incentive to comply with rules. In the real world, moral norms are not perfectly observed. Where moral norms are violated in the real world due to such things as weakness of will, sociopathology, or a misunderstanding of the moral nature of trade, a legal system of some sort can supplement moral norms. However, a legal system by itself is not sufficient for efficiency. I will show that a legal system cannot replace moral normative constraints. Therefore, to the extent that the moral conditions I specify are not met, resources are wasted enforcing compliance and rectifying the results of non-compliance.

In spite of their importance, definite answers to these central questions – much less any kind of consensus – have proved elusive ever since 1776 when Adam Smith in his book, *An Inquiry Into the Nature and Causes of the Wealth of Nations,* claimed that when each person pursues his or her own interests they are together led as if by an *invisible hand* to achieve the common good. Such an achievement requires conventions, but does it also require moral normative constraints? Smith (1776: 456) writes,

As every individual, therefore, endeavors as much as he can both to employ his capital in the support of domestic industry, and so to direct that industry that its produce may be of the greatest value; every individual necessarily labors to render the annual revenue of the society as great as he can. He generally, indeed neither intends to promote the public interest, nor knows how much he is promoting it. By preferring the support of domestic to that of foreign industry, he intends only his own security; and by directing that industry in such a manner as its produce may be of the greatest value, he intends only his own gain, and he is in this, as in many other cases, led by an *invisible hand* to promote an end which was no part of his intention [emphasis added].

It appears that it was not Smith's intention to determine whether, much less which moral normative constraints are required. However, it is certainly understandable that many have understood Smith to assert that, without moral normative constraints, as long as an economic agent "intends *only* his own security" and "*only* his own gain" (emphasis added) that agents will promote some type of common good. That is to say, it is understandable how the claim that legal or moral normative constraints are not necessary could be made on the grounds of Adam Smith's references to an "invisible hand."[3] However, Smith (1776:687) seems to suggest that there is a role for normative constraints in his "obvious and simple system of natural liberty." "Natural liberty" is defined by the absence of governmental interference and by a proviso: "*as long as he does not violate the laws of justice* [emphasis added], [every man] is left perfectly free to pursue his own interest his own way, and to bring both his industry and capital into competition with those of any other man, or order of men." Nevertheless, Smith does not here indicate what he means by "the laws of justice." Nor does he even mention them until Book IV, Chapter IX, far removed from his invisible-hand statement. In his earlier work, *Lectures on Jurisprudence* (1763: 7), Smith writes,

The first and chief design of all civill [sic] governments, is, as I observed, to preserve justice amongst the members of the state and prevent all incroachments [sic] on the individualls [sic] in it, from others of the same society. – {That is, to maintain each individual in his perfect rights.}

Smith divides the set of "perfect rights" into two subsets: natural rights and acquired rights. Natural rights are rights persons hold by virtue of being persons. Natural rights are moral rights. Acquired rights are rights held by virtue of citizenship. Nevertheless, even acquired rights have their basis in morality. Smith (1763: 401) refers to his *A Theory of Moral Sentiments* in his account of the origin of the state to its ground in moral psychology. Thus, for Smith, the "laws of justice" are moral presuppositions of positive law.

Nevertheless, Smith does not show whether or how morality affects the workings of the Invisible Hand. It appears that Smith himself may have recognized that the role of normative constraints in his "system of natural liberty" was not adequately developed in either the first edition of the *Wealth of Nations* or in the earlier *A Theory of Moral Sentiments,* for he spent the last years of his life revising these works to show how the invisible hand is insufficient without morality.[4] I have dealt at length with Adam Smith because it seems that the lack of clarity regarding answers to our central questions can be traced back at least that far.

Contemporary writers who advert to Adam Smith likewise are unclear about the role and specifics of normative constraints for efficient outcomes of market interaction. I am not suggesting that Smith and those who refer to him were attempting to determine whether and which normative constraints are required for efficient outcomes of market interaction. I am drawing attention to how an understanding that efficient outcomes of trade do not require moral normative constraints could be drawn from Smith and others. Consider the account given by Friedman:

Adam Smith's flash of genius was his recognition that the prices that emerged from voluntary transactions between buyers and sellers – for short, in a free market – could coordinate the activity of millions of people, each seeking his own interest, in such a way as to make everyone better off. It was a startling idea then, and it remains one today, that economic order can emerge as the unintended consequences of the actions of many people, each seeking his own interest. (1980:13–4)

It is not clear whether Friedman thinks normative constraints are essential for economically efficient allocations of commodities. The closest Friedman comes to citing anything like normative constraints is the idea that transactions must be voluntary. The concept of voluntary exchange is essential in depicting efficient outcomes of trade, but Friedman does not specify what he means by the term "voluntary." Friedman indicates that voluntariness should be seen primarily as a lack of State coercion – even though he once mentions that robbery is a type of coercion, and once he indicates that people may be coerced by invaders from other nations. But Friedman does not indicate which specific types of normative constraints are required to preclude these kinds of detrimental actions and to ensure that exchanges are voluntary. In all fairness to Friedman, I must reiterate that it is not his explicit intention to specify both the exact meaning of voluntariness and what specific kinds of constraints voluntariness implies.[5] The point is simply that Friedman is not clear regarding both the role and the specific kinds of normative constraints in market interaction. His lack of clarity may depend upon the lack of clarity regarding the notion of a voluntary exchange.

Furthermore, few if any proofs of the First Fundamental Theorem of Welfare Economics (which is commonly understood to be a proof of the Invisible Hand Claim) explicitly indicate the types and role of a system of normative conditions whose effects they presuppose. Furthermore, the First Welfare Theorem along with its assumptions regarding agents has served as a point of departure for legal theory, economic analysis, and moral philosophy in the last two decades of the twentieth century. We have gotten this far in our theorizing without first having achieved some kind of consensus on the moral conditions of economic efficiency.

Morality, Moral Rules, and Normative Constraints

There is also a persistent lack of clarity and of consensus among scholars in philosophy, in economics, and in legal theory regarding some concepts crucial to the central questions we face. Thus, to answer our central questions with sufficient precision, I must stipulate my use of essential terms.

At this point, the concepts of morality and of a normative constraint must be differentiated. In this book, *morality* is understood to be a normative social practice, which is a social phenomenon – a regularity in social behavior – (1) guided by beliefs held in common concerning (a) the criteria by which a group of individuals evaluate their own and others' behavior and according to which criteria they hold each other responsible and (b) the procedures for holding each other responsible, and (2) the purpose of which is directly pertinent to individuals' well-being taken individually and collectively.

The criteria that guide a morality can be rules, norms, or even simple expectations. I use the terms interchangeably even though there are conceptual differences. A person may expect, for instance, that others will not engage in some kinds of behavior, yet it may never have occurred to her to view her expectation as being expressible by rule guiding the behavior of others. Only the notion of criteria guiding behavior is primary. How those criteria themselves are conceptualized is not essential to my argument.

What makes a rule a moral rule is partially a matter of its function in achieving and sustaining well-being through a social practice, where the content of a conception of well-being is dependent on the commonly held beliefs of its correlative community's members.[6] Generally speaking, a particular community's concept of well-being depends on what that community values and how it understands reality, human beings, and the cause of thwarted ideals. Accordingly, to understand the rationale for a moral rule is to understand its relation to these beliefs and to the conception of well-being associated with them.

Furthermore, since a norm, rule, or expectation is moral due to its function in securing a conception of well-being, it follows that what some groups take to be merely a standard of etiquette, others may understand morally – as functioning, that is, to secure well-being. Similarly, what some groups understand to be both legal and moral, others may understand to be legal but not moral, such as the Nuremberg laws in Nazi Germany or the Apartheid laws in pre-democratic South Africa. Further, an obligation to obey the law may be understood by some groups as a moral obligation. Others might believe that a so-called obligation to obey the law is a conceptual mistake or even a redundant[7] legal but not moral obligation. In short, the moral is whatever a particular group sees as such.

Kant's rationale which is supposed to distinguish a rule of morality from a rule of prudence, is an a priori demonstration. But perhaps the differences among a convention, a prudential rule of thumb, and a moral rule are better determined by reference to the types of grounds cited in a rationale. For example, a request for a rationale for a particular convention might elicit the following response:

"That's just the way we do it, that's all. Probably no one knows why."

A rationale for a rule of prudence might go like this:

"If you want to achieve Y, everyone knows that doing X is the only or the best way."

A rationale for a moral rule might, on reflection, refer the interlocutor to what has value, or some feature of human nature.

This account of the moral takes the fact of cultural relativism into consideration. Moralities and their criteria are socially constructed. However, to say that such criteria are socially constructed is not to deny what some groups and traditions hold to be essential about their moral norms. It is not to deny, that is, that their moral rules are either natural laws or God-ordained. It is logically possible that these claims could be true. If so, then the particular social practice guided by such rules is historically situated and takes on the nuances of that situation. Cultural relativism does not imply cognitive relativism.

To reiterate, morality is a social practice guided by moral rules, which in turn are identified as such by virtue of how compliance achieves and sustains communally defined well-being. How, then, does morality and moral rule relate to normative constraint? In the most general sense, a *constraint* is some device that effectively inhibits some type of action from occurring. In economic models of market interaction, agents typically face two kinds of constraints: positive constraints and normative constraints.[8]

Positive constraints delimit a set of physically possible actions. For example, the value of the set of commodities an agent presently holds is her budget constraint. Its value (given in terms of an exchange ratio with other commodities) sets a limit on alternative sets of commodities for which it can be traded. For a simplified example, if Alice has two fish and the value of one fish is either two loaves of bread or one basket of fruit, Alice may trade her fish for four loaves of bread, for two baskets of fruit, or for two loaves of bread and one basket of fruit – but no more. Even though – as we shall see in Chapter 2 – agents in this model prefer a set of commodities having a higher value than the value of the set they presently hold, they cannot purchase such a set. That is, they are positively (or, objectively) prevented from taking an action not because of an enforced rule, but by virtue of a constraint they are powerless to violate.

In contrast, *normative constraints* constitute a broad class of all nonpositive constraints. Normative constraints limit an agent's range of possible actions and are constituted by a norm and a sufficient incentive to comply. Normative constraints involve rules, norms, or behavioral expectations held in common by a group of people, but a normative constraint must be distinguished from a rule, norm, and expectation. A rule proscribing some type of action is not, by itself, a normative constraint. A rule merely expresses a proscription or prescription of some sort. A linguistic expression of a prohibition is not sufficient by itself to preclude the prohibited action. Likewise, merely understanding that certain types of behaviors are required or prohibited is not sufficient to ensure the required behavior or to prevent proscribed behaviors. To have an effect on behavior, a rule must be supplemented (enforced if you will) with a sufficient incentive to comply. In other words, only if a rule is enforced by some mechanism will it have any effect on behavior. An enforcement mechanism supplies an incentive that renders undesirable any action contrary to the rule, thereby inhibiting its occurrence. So, in general, an individual is normatively constrained if and only if she has a sufficient incentive to observe some rule, norm, or behavioral expectation.

Perhaps the following four examples will add more clarity to the concept. First, an individual is normatively constrained if a dictator commands a certain action and enforces it by a threat regarding which the individual has aversive desires, and the individual believes that violations can always be detected. Let the incentive be referred to as an external incentive. Second, an individual is normatively constrained if a legal system proscribes a certain action and enforces it by threats of incarceration or fines regarding which the individual has aversive desires, and the individual believes that violations can always be detected. Again, the individual is normatively constrained by a rule and a sufficient external incentive. Third, an individual is normatively constrained if some moral principle requires some action regarding which the individual has aversive desires, but she values the social "fabric" that the principle preserves over her aversions. In this case the rule is "enforced" by her value for what the rule protects. The incentive in this example is an internal incentive. Finally, an individual is normatively constrained if he observes a rule for no reason other than for duty, or for what he believes about the intrinsic value of following the rules. In these last two cases individuals have an internal incentive to follow the rules, and therefore, in this sense, the rules can be said to be enforced. The point here is to clarify the idea that a normative constraint is constituted by a *rule* (of some type) and either by an external or by a sufficient internal incentive.

Admittedly, the distinction between internal and external incentives is not as precise as it could be. A deeper analysis would show that the intended references of each have both internal and external components. However, for the purposes of answering the two central questions of this book, we need only distinguish between incentives that are purely selfish and those that are not. A purely selfish individual is motivated only to achieve (avoid) his own gain (loss) and to maintain his ability to do so. His gain (loss) is defined solely in terms of his preferences for commodities. A purely selfish agent does not care about the relative satisfaction of others' preferences, much less anything about their relative abilities to lead satisfying lives. By contrast, a non-purely selfish individual cares about others to some degree and the social practices that contribute to their well-being. In this book, purely selfish agents respond to external incentives only, not to internal incentives. I argue that economically efficient outcomes of trade require, among other things, that agents possess internal incentives to comply with a set of moral rules. In this sense, economically efficient outcomes of trade require morality.

In the theoretical model presented in this book, normative constraints are effective because incentives are viewed as always being sufficient. Idealized agents who recognize rules and are universally subject to sufficient motivations can be construed to act in accordance with the rules, even though less than ideal agents may not.

Defining normative constraint in this way entails not only that a rule and some sufficient incentive are necessary, but that they are also sufficient. It may seem that this makes the notion of being normatively constrained a non-normative concept. But it does not. A normative constraint is defined in this book as nonpositive, or non-objective. Recall that a positive, or objective, constraint is a limitation on the set of possible actions about which the agent has no choice regardless of her dispositions or desires. On the other hand, a sufficient incentive depends only on an agent's disposition or desires. Had they been different than they are, the agent could have chosen the alternative course of action. This is exemplified by those people who are naturally disposed to take actions or refrain from actions that norms happen to require or to prohibit. Such norms simply describe their patterns of behavior. From their perspective, they do not feel constrained.

Normative constraints define an agent's admissible strategy domain. Let me explain. The set of actions that are physically possible for an agent is his *natural strategy domain*. The term, *natural strategy domain,* is standard in economics and game theory. But not every physically possible action is rational. Since agents are presumed to be instrumentally rational, the normative constraints of practical reason restrict agents' natural strategy domains and delimit their rational strategy domains. In other words, an agent's *rational strategy domain* is a subset of his or her natural strategy domain. Normative constraints and conventions further restrict individuals' natural strategy domains and delimit agents' admissible strategy domains.

Since an agent's admissible strategy domain is a proper subset of an agent's rational strategy domain, every admissible strategy is also a rational strategy.

Thus, every normative constraint and convention in our model is individually rational. Furthermore, since what makes a rule a moral rule is partially a matter of its function in achieving and sustaining some concept of well-being based on the control beliefs of a given community, moral normative constraints are also collectively rational. I will show that a perfectly competitive market is a normative framework for trade that secures perfect competition and, therefore, is constituted by a set of rational constraints on the pursuit of self-interest.

But the moral rights of a perfectly competitive market are also collectively rational. They result from collective reasoning about goals. There are at least two types of goals. The first type is a completed achievement such as winning the World Series. The second type involves achieving and sustaining some kind of condition, such as getting physically fit. The goal of creating a set of rules to ensure efficient outcomes of market interaction is of the second type. It could go like this:

Premise: We desire to achieve and maintain conditions that ensure economic efficiency.

Premise: Actions of type A undercut our goal, and actions of type B are required.

Conclusion: Therefore, none of us should take an action of type A, which undercuts our goal, and all of us should take actions of type B, which are required.

This piece of reasoning is collectively rational. Even though the question of the rationality of moral constraints in general is thus closely related to central issues in this book, it lies beyond its scope. Nevertheless, since the goal of this book is to specify a system of normative conditions that make efficient outcomes of trade possible, the individual and collective rationality of moral normative constraints is also established.

In sum, morality is a normative social practice, moral rules guide such practices, and a moral normative constraint is a limitation on an agent's range of possible actions and is constituted by a moral rule and a sufficient internal incentive to comply with such norms. Such constraints are both individually and collectively rational.

Synopsis of the Book

In Chapter 2, I develop the theoretical setting required to answer both central questions. I first construct a framework for analyzing social situations.[9] The framework is composed of two divisions corresponding to the two essential aspects of social situations. The first division regards agents; the second, the Situation in which they interact. Agents are depicted in terms of their preferences and their rationality. The Situation within which agents act is defined in terms of positive and normative conditions. Each of the four subcategories (i.e., preferences, rationality, positive conditions, normative conditions) involves at least two variable assumptions. Alternative social situations are, therefore, specified within this framework by variously altering one or more of nine variable assumptions.

By the particular content given to assumptions $(p_1)-(p_5)$, I then specify a particular type of social situation in which agents, who are purely selfish and fully rational, interact in the absence of moral normative constraints; that is, they interact under pure anarchy. I call this particular type of social situation *Strict Rational Egoism*. I have added the adjective, strict, to *rational egoism* to modify egoism so as to indicate pure selfishness in contradistinction to the common term *rational egoism,* which allows altruistic desires and behaviors.

To determine whether moral normative constraints are necessary conditions of efficient outcomes of trade, descriptions of agents must not involve morality in any way, and interaction among agents must not be affected by any morally relevant factors. Thus, for example, such agents must be defined so as to exclude the effects of morally significant constraints such as those attributable to the internalization of moral norms. Therefore, I develop the concept strict rational egoist as a purely selfish agent rather than begin with rational egoists, who are agents who may have preferences that some may view as moral. By specifying the variable assumptions in the framework, I depict Strict Rational Egoism, which is, therefore, a type of social situation in which every agent is a strict rational egoist. A principle of action is derived from Strict Rational Egoism and expresses the necessary and sufficient conditions under which a strict rational egoist will take action.

Notice that I am not attempting to describe or to model actual human behavior. I am modeling the behavior of idealized agents. I show that the absolutely, nonnormatively constrained interaction of such fictitious agents cannot achieve efficient outcomes of trade. Then, I determine at least one set of normative conditions just sufficient to achieve such outcomes. These conditions include a set of moral rules and a change in the agents themselves, which provides internal incentives to comply with the rules. Such incentives are not matters of practical rationality grounded in pure selfishness. They are matters of practical rationality grounded partially, for example, in value for others' well-being or for the social fabric of their lives.[10]

Finally, I further develop the theoretical setting by examining the fact that the presuppositions of the First Fundamental Theorem of Welfare Economics (or First Welfare Theorem) are not the assumptions of Strict Rational Egoism. That is, alternative proofs of the First Welfare Theorem assume either that competitive behavior exists without also indicating the mechanism that ensures it or that the conditions of a perfectly competitive market preclude efficiency-reducing actions. In addition, alternative proofs of the First Welfare Theorem assume the absence of externalities; that is, they assume that there are no intentional, incidental, or accidental effects on the well-being of a consumer or the production possibilities of a firm not accounted for by the market mechanism.[11] Thus, intentional, incidental, and accidental adverse effects on efficiency are presumed not to occur because the actions that cause them are assumed not to be taken. But such effects of agents' actions are not ruled out under Strict Rational Egoism. That is, Strict Rational Egoism does not preclude the possibility of actions being taken that adversely affect the efficiency of outcomes of trade. It does not matter whether such effects are either intentional, incidental, or accidental.

The incompatibility between what the First Welfare Theorem assumes and what Strict Rational Egoism allows points to the ambiguity regarding the role of moral normative constraints in the First Welfare Theorem and underscores the need to examine the role of moral normative constraints.[12] Proofs of the First Fundamental Theorem of Welfare Economics show that under certain conditions every equilibrium allocation of commodities is efficient. But the central question is this: *Must those conditions include moral normative constraints?* If so, then the First Welfare Theorem is not a proof of the common understanding of Adam Smith's claim regarding the Invisible Hand.

By paying close attention to the conditions under which the proof succeeds and by comparing these assumptions to what Strict Rational Egoism allows, we are in a position to determine under what conditions purely selfish agents will engage in trade and achieve efficient outcomes and, thus, to specify the role of morality in the First Welfare Theorem. In versions of the First Welfare Theorem, morality appears to have no role because the actions it precludes are either presumed never to be chosen or else prevented by nonnormative factors. This book clarifies the role and types of normative conditions that the First Welfare Theorem and, by implication, the Invisible Hand Claim presuppose.

In Chapter 3, I make the first of three claims that jointly constitute a response to the first question: *Can a population of strict rational egoists achieve efficient allocations of commodities through market interaction in the absence of moral normative constraints?* On the basis of the specified assumptions of the framework for analyzing social situations, I show that a population of strict rational egoists cannot achieve efficient allocations in the absence of moral normative constraints because moral normative constraints are necessary conditions of competitive behavior. In Chapters 4 and 5, I strengthen the claim by showing that (1) strict rational egoists have no moral incentives to comply with whatever rules are agreed upon and (2) no means exist for internalizing externalities.

There are three reasons why moral normative constraints are necessary conditions. First, a presumption against nonmarket action entails a contradiction. Second, under a widely accepted conception of a "perfectly competitive market," individuals have both an incentive and the means to violate the rules of the process. Therefore, given the *derived principle for action* (DPA), agents will not behave competitively. Finally, even if we alter assumptions (p_5) and (p_6) so that agents have maximal information-processing capabilities and perfect information regarding every economically relevant variable, the possibility exists that no agents will be able to make a decision. In particular, I show that there exists a set of decision functions which are not effectively computable. This section is technical, and the reader may wish to skip to the section summary. Thus, the answer to the first question is that a population of strict rational egoists *cannot* achieve efficient allocations in the absence of moral normative constraints.

In Chapter 4, I strengthen the result by showing that strict rational egoists will not comply with whatever rules are agreed upon. We proceed by way of a response to a possible objection. A spontaneous order objection might be raised against the conclusion of Chapter 3, claiming that the social behavior of selfish individuals in a situation depicted by the specified assumptions of the framework will converge into regular patterns, which, in turn, will be sufficient to produce optimal outcomes of trade. It is important to bear in mind that this is not a denial of the claim that some type of moral normative constraints are necessary conditions of Pareto efficiency. The Spontaneous Order Objection assumes that moral normative constraints are necessary. Rather, it denies that Pareto-optimal equilibrium allocations are not achievable for strict rational egoists in a social situation defined by premises (p_1)–(p_9).

In response to the objection, a rigorous distinction between coordination situations and collective action situations is made, and the role of convention is further developed. We see that conventions are not normative constraints. Furthermore, only moral normative constraints – partially constituted by collective action rules – can converge agents' strategies in collective action situations.

Premises (p_1)–(p_8) define an exchange situation, which is shown to be a collective action situation. After discussing five types of possible solutions to collective action situations, I show that the Spontaneous Order Objection holds only if there is a solution to an exchange situation that arises only from premises (p_1)–(p_8); that is, only if any of the five solutions are internal solutions.

In short, strict rational egoists will not comply with rules because exchange situations are collective action situations, and of the five possible types of solutions to collective action situations, none will be adopted by strict rational egoists. Therefore, the Spontaneous Order Objection fails.

In Chapter 5, I augment the claim that a population of strict rational egoists cannot achieve efficient allocations of commodities through trade by showing that, in the absence of moral normative constraints, no means exist for internalizing externalities. The proof of the First Welfare Theorem implicitly assumes that externalities are absent. Assuming that externalities are absent – just as assuming that every agent behaves competitively – sets the question of the role of normative constraints aside. I first clarify the term *externality* and distinguish between intentional, accidental, and incidental externalities. I show (1) how a specified system of moral normative constraints and procedures (conventions) can secure competitive behavior and can preclude or rectify the effects of the three types of externalities, (2) how moral normative constraints converge expectations and thereby reduce transaction costs, and (3) that moral normative constraints provide logical limits of the commodification of desire. I conclude that since (1) without moral normative constraints, externalities cannot be precluded, much less rectified, (2) that expectations will not converge, and (3) without limits on what kinds of things can be commodified, economic efficiency is not possible for strict rational egoists.

In Chapter 6, I respond to the second question: *What are the moral normative constraints and other normative conditions of market interaction leading to efficient outcomes of trade?* The normative presuppositions of market interaction leading to efficient outcomes include a system of moral normative constraints, a set of conventions for equilibrating supply and demand, and a set of moral normative constraints and conventions for internalizing intentional, accidental, and incidental externalities. The system of moral normative constraints is specified as a normative social practice in which

(i) a set of moral rights – construed as a set of moral Hohfeldian positions that restrict agents' natural and rational strategy domains – provides a moral basis for internalizing externalities,
(ii) each agent has some sufficient internal incentive to comply with these rights, and
(iii) there exists a set of procedures according to which agents hold each other responsible.

Together, the system and the conventions constitute one set of background presuppositions of the First Fundamental Theorem of Welfare Economics.

In Chapter 7, I reiterate and explore the implications of the results for moral philosophy, economics, legal theory, and political theory. In particular I explore and defend the following claims:

Economic Theory

1. A *market* is an institution and *perfect competition* is a type of social interaction secured by a set of normative conditions, which include moral normative constraints and which internalize externalities. A distinction should be maintained between intentional, incidental, and accidental externalities, which are the effects of actions not governed by normative conditions. It follows that a perfectly competitive market includes a set of moral normative constraints and that any proof of the First Welfare Theorem presupposes this general set of normative conditions.

Political Economy and Moral Philosophy

2. The Invisible Hand Claim is mistaken: agents pursuing their interests must also possess internal incentives to comply with a particular set of moral norms to achieve their 'common good'.

Legal Theory

3. Appellate decisions based on economic efficiency must not ignore the moral rights, which are efficiency's necessary conditions.
4. The moral conditions of economic efficiency set moral and logical limits on the commodification of desire.

2

A Contextualized Proof of the First Fundamental Theorem of Welfare Economics

In this chapter, we begin to consider responses to our first question:

Can a population of strict rational egoists achieve efficient allocations of commodities in the absence of moral normative constraints?

To determine the role that moral normative constraints play in the achievement of efficient outcomes of trade, I first develop a framework for analyzing types of social situations. I specify some of the variables in the framework so as to depict a social situation in which moral normative constraints are rigorously excluded. I then present a version of the First Fundamental Theorem of Welfare Economics given a set of standard assumptions under which efficient allocations of commodities are socially achieved. Finally, I compare the assumptions of the First Welfare Theorem with those of the social situation in which moral normative constraints are absent. A thorough understanding of any proof of the First Welfare Theorem must include the role of every relevant assumption. However, my project here is not quite so strong. I only examine some relevant implicit assumptions. My intention is to compare a microeconomic model of social interaction to a model of a specific type of social situation so as to distinguish carefully some, but nevertheless very important, of their respective assumptions.

In the chapters that follow, I argue a Moral Thesis; for strict rational egoists, Pareto-optimal equilibrium allocations of commodities achieved through market interaction are not attainable without moral normative constraints. However, even though proving the Moral Thesis is important in itself, this thesis is not our ultimate objective. It answers only the first question. The ultimate goal is to specify a system of normative conditions that make efficient outcomes of trade possible. In this chapter, we lay down the conceptual groundwork needed to prove the moral thesis and to construct a specific concept of moral normative constraints that make efficient trade possible.

Table 1. *Framework for Situational Analysis*

Type of Social Situation
Agents
Preferences
Rationality
Situation
Positive Conditions
Normative Conditions

A Framework for Analyzing Social Situations

We begin our discussion of the question of whether strict rational egoists can achieve efficient allocations of commodities in the absence of moral normative constraints by developing a framework for analyzing social situations.[1] I do not attempt to make my case from within a microeconomic model or on the basis of game-theoretic models. Rather, I ascertain the presuppositions of the First Welfare Theorem. We need a way to evaluate its explicit and implicit assumptions; thus, we cannot simply begin with existing proofs. Also, we require a way to model rule breaking and rule enforcement, which Ostrom et al. (1994: 25) claimed "cannot be addressed by a non-cooperative game-theoretic model." Since rule breaking and rule enforcement are fundamental issues in this analysis, we have another reason to approach the problem from within a more encompassing framework than has been offered in the past. In short, I take the broadest approach to agents and social situations that is compatible with rigor and clarity.

In this analysis, I adopt a simplified version of the framework developed by Ostrom et al.[2] I use four categories under two broad headings. We refer to an action arena as a *social situation* constituted by agents in a situation. *Agents* are depicted in terms of their *preferences* and their *rationality.* The *situation* is defined in terms of *positive conditions* and *normative conditions.* My framework for analyzing social situations is shown in Table 1.

I next define a particular type of social situation, Strict Rational Egoism, by specifying assumptions falling under each of the four subcategories in this framework.

Strict Rational Egoism

Agents

The basic unit of analysis is the individual agent, rather than groups of agents. This emphasis is in keeping with standard assumptions used in Rational Choice Theory and economic analysis. As James Buchanan (1989: 37) put it,

The central presupposition of any and all rational choice models, including those of the economist, must be the definition of the choosing agent as the individual human being, the unit equipped with some presumed capacity to evaluate options or alternatives and to choose among them. Many of the sophisticated analyses of rationality in choice simply take this presupposition as given, but its central importance should be emphasized. Only individuals choose; only individuals act.

I am, therefore, adopting a form of methodological individualism germane to economic analysis; it is constituted by nine assumptions. My first assumption regarding agents themselves is this:

(p_1) Each agent's preferences range over alternative social states defined solely in terms of their own consumption bundles.

I will use the terms *social state, state of affairs, social situation,* and *outcome* interchangeably. I intend the terms to be nearly identical in meaning to both Amartya Sen's (1970a, 1992) and Jules Coleman's (1992) "social states." Sen (1970a: 152) defined a *social state* as a "complete description of society."[3] I understand Sen's social state to be a maximal state of affairs. A maximal state of affairs is described by a list of every true proposition at a point in time. A *social state,* as I will use the term, is a maximal state of affairs in this sense.

Having described the concept of a social state, let me now add one caveat: Only a subset of the aspects of any social state are relevant to any individual. It would be impossible and unnecessary for any agent to imagine, much less completely describe, even one social state. So even though a social state is a maximal state of affairs, when we portray agents as choosing from a set of alternative social states,[4] we imagine them as taking into consideration only those aspects that affect their decisions; those aspects being alternative consumption bundles.

A *consumption bundle* is a set of commodities that some agent could consume and is specified by a list of the amount of each commodity in the set. Hence, a social state is described in terms of a distribution of consumption bundles. For example, an agent might choose a social state in which he gets two loaves of bread and one fish. What anyone else gets is irrelevant to purely selfish agents. A complete description of a social state mentions every individual's consumption bundle.

Preferences should be understood in terms of a relation between social states. Individuals are able to say whether, for any two social states, he or she *prefers* one over the other or is indifferent. Therefore, for any subset of social states we assume that agents compare each alternative to every other alternative, thereby generating a preference relation. To illustrate these concepts, suppose that in some social state – name it #1 – Ida's consumption bundle is comprised of four loaves of bread and one fish; in social state #2, Ida's consumption bundle is three loaves and two fish; and in social state #3, one loaf and four fish. Comparing every alternative pair, Ida prefers #2 to #1, #1 to #3, and #2 to #3. Thus, we have a list of Ida's preferences.

Let me now describe how to model this mathematically. A *preference relation* is a binary relation (i.e., set of ordered pairs) defined on a subset of social states. Let the uppercase italicized letter Z represent the set of every alternative social state. Think of this as representing the range of outcomes that would result from an agent taking any possible alternative course of action. Each individual social state is represented by the lower-case Greek letter σ_n followed by a subscript representing its index number. Thus, $Z = \{\sigma_1, \ldots, \sigma_n\}$. Now let A be a subset of Z, that is, $A \subseteq Z$. Ida's preference relation, R_{Ida}, is $\{(\sigma_2, \sigma_1), (\sigma_1, \sigma_3), (\sigma_2, \sigma_3)\}$. In general, let the letter I represent the set of individuals, $i \in I = \{1, \ldots, n\}$, let i be the name of a single individual, and let R be a preference relation. Thus, $R_i = \{(\sigma_m, \sigma_n): i$ thinks that σ_m is at least as good as $\sigma_n\}$. I will further discuss the preference relation when I discuss assumption (p_2). But first I want to clarify some important implications of (p_1).[5]

As I mentioned in Chapter 1, Adam Smith was unclear regarding morally relevant influences on agents' actions, and it remains an issue of debate among Smith scholars whether his understanding of the invisible hand involved such influences. Moreover, few if any proofs of the First Welfare Theorem show the role of a system of normative conditions. To determine what agents can achieve by complying with a set of rules and procedures, we must first determine what they can achieve in the complete absence of morally relevant influences on their actions. We must examine a model in which interactions among agents are not affected by moral considerations of any kind.[6] In this analysis, morality is understood to be a *normative social practice* that is a social phenomenon – a regularity in social behavior – (1) guided by beliefs held in common (a) concerning the criteria by which a group of individuals evaluate their own and others' behavior and according to which criteria they hold each other responsible and (b) concerning the procedures for holding each other responsible, and (2) the purpose of which is directly pertinent to individuals' well-being. Therefore, morally relevant influences on behavior are modeled as *moral normative constraints,* each constituted by a rule and a sufficient internal incentive to comply. We retain the idea that agents prefer social states, but the way those states are achieved is relevant to which ones are sought. Moral agents seek only those social states that are achieved justly because moral normative constraints restrict the range of alternative means to achieve social states.

However, for strict rational egoists, there exist no internally motivated, morally significant effects on behavior. I accomplish this in (p_1) by indicating that preferences range only over alternative social states defined solely in terms of consumption bundles. Note that assumption (p_1) also implies that agents' preferences do not range over alternative visions of society as a whole, character types, decision rules, others' attitudes, or the relative satisfaction of others' goals.

I treat agents' actions as purposive in that they act so as to achieve a goal.[7] There are two types of goals from which individuals can possibly derive some satisfaction. The first type of goal is a social state defined in terms of a consumption bundle. This type of goal is central to our model. We are working to isolate and understand this feature of a theory of individual behavior.

We must preclude a second kind of goal: the goal of sustaining a particular kind of social condition or personal attribute. Such must be precluded because it involves a morally relevant constraint on actions. For example, an individual may prefer some particular vision of how society should function, act accordingly, and attempt to persuade and recruit others to the same vision. An agent, for example, might prefer to develop and sustain a certain type of character or reputation regardless of what others do. An ancient Hebrew proverb reads, "a good name is to be desired above fine gold." Pursuing this type of goal, an individual aspires to sustain a sequence of states of affairs characterized in part by her exhibiting this character description. The agent may reason that such a goal is achieved by performing some types of actions and refraining from other types. She then adopts the appropriate rules that require or forbid such actions. Such rules become morally significant constraints in that the agent knows that if she takes certain actions she will adversely affect her own character goal. My model, Strict Rational Egoism, excludes such constraints.

Preferences for social states achieved by observing a set of explicit and accepted decision rules can also have morally significant effects on agents' actions. An agent may develop some set of supplementary decision rules that help to sort out alternative means to achieve social states. The utility maximization criterion [which I describe under assumption (p_3)] and some other kinds of supplementary decision rules do not rule out actions that have adverse effects on efficiency, such as theft and fraud. Moreover, it might not be possible to ascertain whether such decision rules might indirectly rule out such actions. Even if the utility maximization criterion and supplementary decision rules could indirectly preclude actions having adverse effects on efficiency, it is irrelevant to the goal of this analysis. We are concerned with the role of moral normative constraints that directly rule out adverse actions; therefore, we must rule out decision rules that are moral principles, precluding the possibility that an agent may unilaterally and rationally elect to act on some set of moral principles. For example, an agent either takes an action or refrains from taking it either because he generalizes his prospective action in accordance with something like Kant's Categorical Imperative or because he calculates his alternatives looking for which action generates the greatest happiness or because it violates his understanding of the principle of justice.

Finally, individuals' behavior can be affected when their preferences range over others' *attitudes* such as approval or disapproval or over the relative satisfaction of others' preferences. Therefore, my model stipulates that individuals do not have altruistic, sadistic, or even meddlesome attitudes toward others. Individuals do not care about others. Individuals do not care whether others approve of them or are successful in satisfying their own goals. Therefore, individuals do not help or hinder anyone else due to the satisfaction or dissatisfaction they might possibly receive regarding others' achievements.

In sum, I want to specify the nature and object of agents' preferences, but I also want rigorously to exclude any effects of morally relevant factors. By assumption (p_1), I have stipulated that preferences range over alternative social states defined only by alternative consumption bundles. Assumption (p_1) implies that preferences do not range over alternative visions of society as a whole, character types, or decision rules. It also implies that preferences do not range over others' attitudes or the relative satisfaction of others' goals or any other types of considerations that I may have missed.

Here again is the difference between rational egoism as commonly understood and Strict Rational Egoism: We must eliminate any factor that is either obviously morally relevant or else possibly conceivable as such, to determine first what purely selfish agents can accomplish in the absence of moral normative constraints.

The second assumption I make about agents is this:

(p_2) Agents' preference relations are stable, rational, and locally non-satiated.

The preference relation is assumed to remain *stable* over time. This simply means that an agent's goals are not dependent on time; that is, the reasons individuals choose a particular goal do not change as a function of the passage of time. This assumption enables prediction and prevents attributing anomalies to "inexplicable" changes in individuals' dispositions.[8]

Each individual's preference relation is *rational*. A preference relation is *rational* if and only if the preference relation is complete and transitive.[9] A preference relation is *complete* if and only if any two social states can be compared and ranked. A preference relation is *transitive* if and only if, for any three social states, σ_k, σ_n, and σ_m, if σ_k is preferred to σ_n and σ_n is preferred to σ_m, then σ_k is preferred to σ_m.

We might assume that, in general, each agent prefers more of any given commodity than less. That is, we might say that for any two consumption bundles, x and y, if y has at least as much of every commodity as x, but more of at least one commodity, then y is strictly preferred to x. In this case, the preference relation is strictly monotone. This assumption is sufficient when all commodities are desirable. However, some commodities are undesirable, such as contaminated water, and others such as extremely rich desserts are undesirable in amounts beyond a certain size. For these reasons, we replace the strictly monotone condition with local nonsatiation.

Assumptions (p_1) and (p_2) pertain to individuals' preferences. Assumptions (p_3)–(p_5) define individuals' rationality. An agent's goal is to reach the most preferred feasible outcome. I represent an agent's rationality in choosing that goal as follows:

(p_3) Agents' goals are selected according to a utility maximization criterion.

To say that an agent chooses from a set of alternative social states is simply to say that he chooses from a set of alternative goals. A purely selfish agent seeks to maximize his utility. *Utility* is an ordinal or purely comparative measure of satisfaction an individual receives from achieving a preferred social state. We may look at it as a measure of how well-off an individual is under a particular social state. In other words, utility is a measure of well-being or welfare. An agent maximizes utility if and only if he achieves that state of affairs that yields the highest level of utility, that is, the most preferred state of affairs. Thus, each individual's selection criterion is utility maximization.

The second assumption regarding agents' rationality is this:

(p_4) Agents' beliefs depend only on information.

An individual's choice of a course of action depends upon the information she has regarding alternative states of affairs and the relative effectiveness of alternative actions believed sufficient to achieve them. We describe in more detail the information constraints each agent faces under assumption (p_6). We discuss individuals' information-processing capabilities under assumption (p_5). We note here that decisions made by strict rational egoists depend only on information and not on habit or irrational behavior.

We assume that individuals are sufficiently capable of assessing the situation they face and of choosing the best course of action to reach their goals. It is expressed by this assumption:

(p_5) Agents are sufficiently and instrumentally rational.

An *instrumentally* rational person chooses the course of action that achieves the outcome that maximizes utility while expending the least amount of resources. Thus, actions are the "instruments" by which individuals achieve their goals.

A Derived Principle for Action

To justify the claims we make about the types of actions individuals either will or will not take, we require a principle that states the necessary and sufficient conditions under which an agent so construed will take action. Instrumental rationality is axiomatic and forms the basis of the following provisional version of a principle for action (where action a_n^i denotes person i's nth option):

For any person i, action a_n^i, and state of affairs σ_n,
i will take a_n^i if and only if
    (i) i's goal is σ_n and
    (ii) a_n^i is the best means to achieve σ_n.

(I will use the phrases "i's goal is σ_n" and "i prefers σ_n" synonymously to mean person i takes social state σ_n as his or her goal social state, i.e., as the most highly ranked alternative social state.)

Now, suppose that – for any non-moral reason – action a_n^i cannot be taken. For example, that action a_n^i – under these conditions – is physically impossible. We note that a proposed means must be feasible so we stipulate that a_n^i is the best feasible means.

However, what if (for any reason) i does not believe that action a_n^i is the best feasible means? In that case, we revise the principle as follows: "i believes that a_n^i is the best . . ."; however, that revision leaves open the possibility that action a_n^i may not be the best means. Furthermore, when information is asymmetrically distributed, person i may not know what actions are the best. Our principle must, therefore, allow for the possibility that i could be mistaken but that the mistakes are not due to errors in reasoning. We amend the principle, therefore, to indicate that i has good reason to believe that a_n^i is the best means. If it turns out that a_n^i is physically impossible, i will not take a_n^i and will wait for an alternative set of opportunities. So we stipulate that "i has good reason to believe that a_n^i is the best feasible means."

Notice that seldom, if ever, is a single action sufficient to achieve a certain state of affairs. It often requires several distinct and related actions. Alternatively, we could denote a course of action, $a_1^i, \ldots, a_n^i$. So let action a_n^i denote a course of action that may have only one element. Hence, we have the following derived principle for action which applies to *strict rational egoists:*

DPA: For any person i, action a_n^i, and state of affairs σ_n,
       i will take a_n^i if and only if
          (i) i prefers σ_n, and
          (ii) i has good reason to believe that a_n^i is the best feasible
             means to achieve σ_n.[10]

Situation

We want to specify as much as is necessary the conditions under which agents will engage in trade. In addition to the characteristics of individuals themselves, we must consider the conditions presented by the situation in which individuals interact. Whenever agents interact in social situations, they face some set of conditions that defines the initial situation in which they find themselves and that determines their strategy domains. The situation is, thus, defined by certain kinds of physical circumstances and by particular types of socially constructed conditions. I refer to relevant physical circumstances as *positive constraints* and to the socially constructed conditions as *normative conditions*. The first assumptions I make regarding the situation in which agents interact is the following positive constraint:

> (p$_6$) Agents are constrained by a perfectly competitive market: numerous participants, homogeneous products, freedom of exit and entry, and perfect information.

A *perfectly competitive market* includes numerous participants, homogeneous products, freedom of exit and entry, and perfect information.[11] The assumption of numerous individuals is supposed to ensure that the decisions of a single buyer or seller cannot significantly affect price. The assumption of homogeneity of product indicates that products do not vary within types so that there can be no product-based incentive to purchase from one seller rather than another. We specify the freedom of entry and exit assumption by indicating that sellers face no *natural* barriers either to enter the market or to exit the market. We need not assume that sellers face no *artificial* barriers erected by some sort of coalition of agents. Since the activity of a coalition depends on some sort of agreement (explicit or tacit) between its members, admitting the existence of coalitions entails admitting the existence of a normative structure into the model.

Agents also face constraints imposed by a relative distribution and quality of information. We assume that individuals have perfect information regarding every economically relevant variable except the preference relations and the natural strategy domains of others. In other words, each agent knows all the factors relevant to his own decision and such knowledge is distributed symmetrically; that is, everyone has the same information.

The second assumption I make regarding the positive conditions that individuals face is this:

> (p$_7$) Agents control finite resources.

We assume an initial distribution of goods that render to each agent an initial endowment. Each agent's endowment is finite. (Each agent's natural strategy domain is thereby constrained.) However, we must assume a barter economy since to assume money as a medium of exchange is to introduce norms (other than the norms of practical rationality) into the assumption set.[12] Prices in a barter market are simply the bundles of alternative goods that a seller is willing to accept and a buyer is willing to pay.

To answer our central questions, we must model a social situation in which there are no enforced rules or social roles having corresponding obligations or privileges except conventions that equilibrate supply and demand.[13] It is not simply the case that rules are not enforced. There are no moral rules to enforce. Elinor Ostrom et al (1994: 77–8) argued that a precise study of interaction situations requires a "common, theoretical language of rules." An action situation involves a set of constitutive rules which the authors call a *rule configuration.* The authors adduce seven types of constitutive rules: position, boundary, authority, aggregation, scope, information, and payoff. "Rules that affect the set of actions available to a player, for example, are classified as authority rules" and "[r]ules that directly affect the benefits and costs assigned to actions and outcomes are payoff rules, and so on" (1994: 77). A description of a rule configuration then is equivalent to a description of a normative constraint set. Normative conditions effectively delimit the range of possible outcomes an agent may pursue by limiting the possible types of actions she may take. The set of possible outcomes is the *opportunity set.* What Ostrom et al. referred to as the *configural nature of rules* (1994: 77) is the fact that the opportunity set can be affected by more than one rule. Therefore, to examine a social situation precisely, one needs to examine the full rule configuration.

However, the specification of the full rule configuration requires both a set of physical statements and a set of deontological statements (i.e., statements that indicate which actions are obligatory, permitted, or prohibited).[14] But where agents' actions are not constrained by rules,[15] the specification of the normative conditions category requires that a default condition be specified. Since we are working to specify market interaction unconstrained by norms, we specify a default condition. The default condition that indicates the absence of such rules is a default authority condition. It indicates that "[e]ach player may take any physically possible action" (1994: 78). These considerations are expressed or entailed by my final assumptions:

(p$_8$) There are no moral rules.

(p$_9$) There are conventions to equilibrate supply and demand.

Standards of Evaluation of Outcomes

Alternative allocations of commodities define alternative social states. Thus, an agent's goal is defined solely in terms of his most highly valued consumption bundle. Outcomes of social interaction are social states and are evaluated in terms of how successful agents are *as a group* in achieving their respective goals. Standards for evaluating outcomes measure the relative level of success such agents realize in achieving their goals. There are several such standards. I use Pareto standards primarily because they are used in virtually every proof of the First Welfare Theorem, also known as the Invisible Hand Theorem.[16]

Pareto Optimal. A feasible social state is Pareto optimal if and only if there is no possible alternative social state that is Pareto superior to it.

Pareto Superior. A social state σ_1 is Pareto superior to σ_2 if and only if at least one person is better off (measured in terms of more of at least one commodity) under σ_1 than under σ_2 and no one is worse off.

Thus, a feasible social state σ_1 is Pareto optimal if and only if there is no social state σ_2 such that at least one person is better off under σ_2 than under σ_1 and no one is worse off under σ_2 than under σ_1.

Notice that Pareto standards apply to social states, not preferences. A standard for evaluating preferences is inappropriate, since that would introduce moral considerations into the model. We simply take preferences as given. We follow Vanberg (1994) and refer to this view as normative individualism.

Summary

The background assumptions of our framework for analyzing social situations are shown in Table 2. We have been developing a framework that will enable us to consider the research question: Can a population of strict rational egoists achieve efficient allocations of commodities in the absence of moral normative constraints? Assumptions (p_1)–(p_9) specify the variables in the framework so as to depict Strict Rational Egoism – a social situation in which morally relevant constraints are rigorously excluded. In particular, the influence of internal

Table 2. *Strict Rational Egoism*

Agents

Preferences

(p1) Each agent's preferences range over alternative social states defined solely in terms of their own consumption bundles.

(p2) Agents' preference relations are stable, rational, and locally nonsatiated.

Rationality

(p3) Agents' goals are selected according to a utility maximization criterion.

(p4) Agents' beliefs depend only on information.

(p5) Agents are sufficiently and instrumentally rational.

Situation

Positive Conditions

(p6) Agents are constrained by a perfectly competitive market: numerous participants, homogeneous products, freedom of exit and entry, and perfect information.

(p7) Agents control finite resources.

Normative Conditions:

(p8) There are no moral rules.

(p9) There are conventions to equilibrate supply and demand.

morally relevant factors is precluded by assumption (p_1). The influence of external morally relevant factors is precluded by assumptions (p_8).

A Proof of the First Fundamental Theorem of Welfare Economics

A Pure Exchange Economy

For this version of the First Welfare Theorem, we consider a Pure Exchange Model of trade. Imagine that agents either hunt, gather, or farm during a six-day period. Agents are self-sufficient "Robinson Crusoes" who produce and consume for themselves. While each of the three types of commodities associated with each activity are available throughout the region in which the population dwells, there exists a variation in distribution in each type. The result is that there also exists a variation in the amount of effort it takes to acquire a given commodity.

At one location on a certain day once every week, each agent is free to trade (if she so desires) some of what she has for other commodities that she desires more. Prices are exchange ratios. In other words, the price of a unit of one commodity is a number of units of another commodity. Thus, to acquire a certain amount of one type of commodity, agents give up or trade set amounts of other commodities. The price of a loaf of bread, for example, may be one fish. No agent can affect prices except through the conventions of a price mechanism. In this case, agents take prices as they are given by a *Walrasian auctioneer*[17] who, in the presence of all prospective traders, calls out a set of prices. Each trader then, on the basis of his preferences, determines what amount of each commodity he is willing to buy or sell at those prices and reports this to the auctioneer. Unless all commodities that agents desire to sell are sold and all commodities that agents desire to buy are acquired, the auctioneer calls out a revised set of prices – lowering (raising) the exchange ratio on those unsold commodities (commodities not offered for sale).

Agents and Commodities

Each agent possesses a determinate amount of goods on the day of trade.

Definition. There are m commodities, and each is denoted by some $j \in \mathbb{N} = \{1, \ldots, m\}$.

Definition. There are n consumers (i.e., agents), and each is denoted by some $i \in \mathbb{N} = \{1, \ldots, n\}$.

Definition. Let:

x_j^i denote each agents i's *prospective or final quantity* x of good j, and
w_j^i denote each agents i's *initial quantity* of good j on the day of trade.

Each agent's preferences range over alternative social states, which are defined solely in terms of some amount of a combination of goods to be consumed.

Definition. A *consumption bundle of agent i* is an m-vector belonging to i's *consumption set* and is denoted by $(x_1^i, \ldots, x_m^i) = x^i.$[18]

Thus, to refer to some commodity j in some specific consumption bundle x^i, controlled by some agent i, we write: x_j^i. To differentiate between consumption bundles of one agent, we will use x^i, y^i, and z^i.

Finally, each agent is depicted as having an *initial endowment* construed as an initial consumption bundle that is brought to market.

Definition. For each agent i, let $w^i = (w_1^i, \ldots, w_m^i)$ alternatively denote each agents i's *initial consumption bundle*.

The Preference Relation

We have defined a preference relation as a set of ordered pairs of social states characterized only by consumption bundles. We may therefore depict the preference relation in terms of consumption bundles only, as is common practice in proofs of the First Welfare Theorem. Accordingly, we define three kinds of preference relations as follows:

$\succcurlyeq_i =$ {(x,y): agent i *weakly prefers* x to y, that is, i thinks that x is at least as good as y},

$\succ_i =$ {(x,y): agent i *strictly prefers* x to y}, and

$\approx_i =$ {(x,y): agent i is *indifferent* between x and y}.

Definition. $\forall x,y \; [x \succ_i y \Leftrightarrow x \succcurlyeq_i y \; \& \; \neg(y \succcurlyeq_i x)]$

Definition. $\forall x,y \; [x \approx_i y \Leftrightarrow x \succcurlyeq_i y \; \& \; (y \succcurlyeq_i x)]$

We make several important assumptions about each agent's preferences; these assumptions affect the choices they make. Since agents are rational, they will not trade themselves into poverty. Thus, we specify the following:

For any consumption bundles, x^i, y^i, or z^i,

$\succcurlyeq_i$ is *complete* iff $x^i \succcurlyeq_i y^i$ or $y^i \succcurlyeq_i x^i$,

$\succcurlyeq_i$ is *transitive* iff $x^i \succcurlyeq_i y^i$ and $y^i \succcurlyeq_i z^i$, then $x^i \succcurlyeq_i z^i$.

In general, agents prefer more of any given commodity to less. We want this to be represented in agents i's preference relation. Therefore, we say that for any two consumption bundles, x^i and y^i, if y^i has more of at least one commodity, then y^i is strictly preferred to x^i and that $\succcurlyeq_i$ is *locally nonsatiated*.

For our purposes, the following definition is more explicit and more adequate in a pure exchange economy:

Definition

(1) Let $x = (x^1, \ldots, x^n)$ and $y = (y^1, \ldots, y^n)$ be two consumption bundles.

(2) An agent i is said to be *selfish* if he or she only cares about his or her components of allocations, so that a preference relation $x \succcurlyeq_i y$ is equivalent to (and may be written as) $x^i \succcurlyeq_i y^i$; similarly, $x \succ_i y$ can be written as $x^i \succ_i y^i$. In a pure exchange economy, absence of externalities is synonymous with all agents being selfish.

(3) A selfish consumer i with preference relation $\succcurlyeq_i$ is said to be *locally nonsatiated* if and only if for every $x^i = (x^i_1, \ldots, x^i_m)$ and for every number $\varepsilon > 0$, there is some other consumption bundle $y^i = (y^i_1, \ldots, y^i_m)$ such that

  (i) $\|x^i_j - y^i_j\| \le \varepsilon$ for every $j = 1, \ldots, m$, and

  (ii) $y^i \succ_i x^i$.

Other Definitions

Definition. A *consumption allocation* $x = (x^1, \ldots, x^n)$ is a complete list of consumption bundles for a population of n consumers.

It is not possible in this economy to have a negative amount of any commodity, but all nonnegative commodity bundles are assumed to be individually feasible; nor is it possible to increase the total amount of some commodity by trading; neither can goods be disposed of freely (the "no free disposal" assumption).

Definition. In a pure exchange economy, an allocation $x = (x^1, \ldots, x^n)$, $x^i = (x^i_1, \ldots x^i_m)$, is *feasible* iff

(1) $\forall i,j, \ x^i_j \ge 0$, and

(2) $\forall i,j, \ \left[\sum_{i=1}^{n} x^i_j = \sum_{i=1}^{n} w^i_j \right]$.[19]

Definition. The real numbers p_r, $r \in M = \{1, \ldots, m\}$ are said to be the *nonnormalized prices* of commodity k, if goods $j \in M$, $k \in M$ are exchanged in ratio: p_j/p_k.

Definition. A *nonnormalized price vector*, $p = (p_1, \ldots, p_m)$, is a list of real numbers representing the exchange ratios between alternative commodities.

A consumption bundle $y^i = (y^i_1, \ldots, y^i_m)$ is *affordable* to agent i if its total cost does not exceed agent i's wealth w^i, which, in a pure exchange economy, is the value of i's initial endowment given a price vector p.

Definition. An individually feasible consumption bundle $y^i = (y^i_1, \ldots, y^i_m)$, $y^i_j \in \mathbb{R}_+$, is *affordable* iff $py^i \leq pw^i$,

where $py^i = (p_1 y^i_1 + \cdots + p_m y^i_m)$, and
where w^i is ith agent's initial endowment.

We shall assume that $w^i \geq 0$, for all i.

Definition. A budget set $B^i_{pw} = \{y^i \in C^i : py^i \leq pw^i\}$ is the set of all affordable consumption bundles for some agent i with endowment w^i, given a price vector p.

Definition. A selfish agent i *maximizes satisfaction competitively* if and only if

(1) i obtains $y^i \in B^i_{pw}$ such that $\neg \exists\, z \in B^i_{pw}: z^i >_i y^i$, and
(2) agent i is a price-taker.[20]

Definition. In a pure exchange economy, assuming all agents to be selfish, a price vector p^* (i.e., a list of prices – one for each commodity) and an allocation x^* (i.e., a list of consumption bundles x^{*i} – one for each individual i) is a *competitive equilibrium* if and only if

(1) each agent i maximizes satisfaction competitively at the bundle x^{*i} when p^* prevails, and
(2) the allocation x^* is feasible.

x^* is called a *competitive equilibrium allocation*.

We are interested in efficient outcomes of trade, which are called Pareto-optimal allocations of commodities. An allocation of commodities defines a social state. Pareto optimality is defined as follows:

Pareto Optimal. A feasible social state (feasible allocation) A is Pareto optimal if and only if there is no feasible social state (feasible allocation) B such that at least one person is better off under B than under A and no one is worse off under B than under A.

Notice that saying, "one person is better off under B than under A," is by definition equivalent to saying, "one person prefers B to A." But a selfish agent prefers some allocation B over another A if and only if he or she prefers his or her consumption bundle in B over his or her consumption bundle in allocation A. We may, therefore, formally translate Pareto optimality as follows:

Definition. In a pure exchange economy – assuming all agents to be selfish – a feasible allocation $z = (z^1, \ldots, z^n)$ is *Pareto optimal* if and only if there is no other feasible allocation $y = (y^1, \ldots, y^n)$ such that

(1) for at least one agent i, $y^i >_i z^i$, and
(2) for each agent r, $y^r \geqslant_i z^r$.

Theorem. *In a pure exchange economy, if there are no externalities and preferences are locally non-satiated, then every competitive equilibrium allocation z^* is Pareto optimal.*

Proof.[21]

(1) Let (z^*, p^*) be a competitive equilibrium, and suppose $z^* = (z^1, \ldots, z^n)$ is a competitive equilibrium allocation that is not Pareto optimal. Since by *"competitive equilibrium allocation"* $=_{df} z^* = (z^1, \ldots, z^n)$ is feasible, and since by *"feasible"* $=_{df}$, $\forall j$, $[\sum_{i=1}^{n} Z_j^i = \sum_{i=1}^{n} W_j^i]$, the total value of $z^* = (z^1, \ldots, z^n)$ at price vector p^* is equal to the total value of $w = (w^1, \ldots, w^n)$, at p^*. That is,

$$(2)\ \sum_{i=1}^{n} p * z^{*i} = \sum_{i=1}^{n} p * w^i.$$

Since z^* is not Pareto optimal, there is some other feasible allocation $y = (y^1, \ldots, y^n)$ preferred by at least one agent and not dispreferred by others. That is,

(3) $\exists$ feasible $y = (y^1, \ldots, y^n)$ and $i \in \{1, \ldots, n\}$ such that
    (3.1) $y^i >_i z^{*i}$, and
    (3.2) $y^r \geqslant_r z^{*r}, \forall r \in \{1, \ldots, n\}$

[In (3.1) and (3.2) preference relations are between consumption bundles. This is meaningful because, by the assumption of absence of externalities, each agent is selfish.]

Since each agent's preference relation is locally nonsatiated, the total value of $y = (y^1, \ldots, y^n)$ exceeds[22] that of $w = (w^1, \ldots, w^n)$, i.e.,

$$(4)\ \sum_{i=1}^{n} p * y^i > \sum_{i=1}^{n} p * w^i.$$

But since by definition, $y = (y^1, \ldots, y^n)$ is feasible, the total value of $y = (y^1, \ldots, y^n)$ is equal to the total value of $w = (w^1, \ldots, w^n)$.

$$(5)\ \sum_{i=1}^{n} p * y^i = \sum_{i=1}^{n} p * w^i.$$

But (5) contradicts (4). Hence, z^* is Pareto optimal.   Q.E.D.

Summary Discussion

We conclude that every equilibrium allocation is Pareto optimal, given the assumptions as they are stated in this section regarding commodities, agents, and the conventions under which they engage in trade. However, this proof depends on a set of assumptions that differs from the assumptions comprising Strict Rational Egoism, $(p_1) - (p_9)$, in two subtle, but essential respects. First of all, in this proof an equilibrium allocation is a competitive equilibrium allocation. In this proof, by definition, an allocation is an equilibrium allocation only if every individual maximizes utility competitively. And by definition every individual maximizes utility competitively only if he or she is a price-taker. Price-taking (i.e., competitive behavior) implies, for example, that no agent chooses to misrepresent the quantities of commodities he is willing to sell in order to affect price levels to his own advantage, or that no individual gives false information when the opportunity presents itself as a best means to maximize utility. In other words, certain actions, which adversely affect the efficiency of outcomes, are *presumed* never to be the best means for an agent to achieve his goals. Moral normative constraints play no part because the actions they preclude are presumed never to be chosen.

Second, this proof explicitly assumes that externalities are absent. Mas-Colell et al. (1995: 352) define *externality* as follows:

An *externality* is present whenever the well-being of a consumer or the production possibilities of a firm are directly affected by the actions of another agent in the economy.

This definition omits important elements. The following definition is better:

Externality. An *externality* is the effect of some action related to production or consumption that imposes an involuntary cost or benefit on some other agent and for which no compensation is made.

Moreover, externalities are usually understood as being the incidental effects of the acts of production and consumption. But the effects of acts of theft or fraud and the harm inflicted through negligence are also externalities and exemplify intentional and accidental effects on the well-being of some individual. Therefore, assuming that externalities are absent – just as assuming that every agent behaves competitively – sets the question of the role of morality or law aside because it assumes that all these types of externalities do not occur.

Notice that there is some overlap in the work being done by both assumptions: both exclude what we refer to as intentional externalities.

Conversely, if it can be shown how a specified system of moral normative constraints and conventions can secure competitive behavior and rectify the effects of accidental and incidental externalities so that individuals can achieve

Pareto optimal equilibrium allocations, the question of the role of morality will be clarified and advanced.

In this chapter, I have described a framework for analyzing types of social situations to depict a social situation in which moral normative constraints are rigorously excluded and have presented a proof the First Welfare Theorem taking note of the differences between the assumptions of the proof and those of the framework. The centerpiece of the framework is the idea of a strict rational egoist – an agent wholly unaffected by morally relevant factors. In Chapters 3 through 6 I offer arguments demonstrating that strict rational egoists cannot achieve efficient outcomes of trade.

3

The Moral Thesis

Moral Normative Constraints Are Necessary Conditions of Pareto-Optimal Equilibrium Allocations of Commodities Achieved through Market Interaction

Chapters 3 through 6 are dedicated to answering the first central question:

> *Can a population of strict rational egoists achieve efficient allocations of commodities through market interaction in the absence of moral normative constraints?*

In this chapter, I argue for a Moral Thesis regarding economic efficiency:

> Moral normative constraints are necessary conditions of Pareto-optimal equilibrium allocations of commodities achieved through market interaction.

Pareto-optimal allocations of goods require moral normative constraints because these outcomes of market interaction require perfect competition, and moral normative constraints are necessary for perfect competition. More technically, a proof of the First Fundamental Theorem of Welfare Economics establishes that efficient allocations of goods depend on every individual maximizing utility competitively. By definition, an agent maximizes utility competitively if and only if she attempts to obtain that consumption bundle within her budget constraint such that no other bundle is more preferred, and price-taking is the best course of action to achieve her goal. Therefore, the validity of the theorem depends on competitive behavior, and competitive behavior is secured by moral normative constraints.

I will treat the terms *price-taking behavior, competitive behavior,* and *market behavior* synonymously. *Price-taking* is a type of market action defined partially by an agent's belief that she cannot affect price levels. She makes her trading decisions entirely based on announced prices. All behavior that leads to inefficiency I refer to as *noncompetitive* or *nonmarket* behavior. I use the terms *force (theft)* and *fraud* to differentiate two broad classes of noncompetitive behavior. *Fraud* covers types of action in which, for example, an agent chooses to misrepresent the quantities of commodities he is willing to sell to affect price levels to his own advantage. Consider also an individual who, when the opportunity presents itself, gives false information as a best means to maximize utility.

Stated more precisely, my immediate task is to show that, in addition to the conventions of a price mechanism for equilibrating supply and demand, a system of moral normative constraints is necessary to secure competitive behavior. This task is logically equivalent to showing that it is false that there are no moral normative constraints and that individuals behave competitively. Since our framework for analyzing social situations indicates that there are no moral rules and that strict rational egoists have no internal incentives to act morally, the Moral Thesis is proved if such individuals will not behave competitively under Strict Rational Egoism.

Although there exist arguments that some system of rules is required for efficiency, a proof of adequate precision and specificity showing why purely selfish agents cannot achieve efficient outcomes of trade in the absence of moral normative constraints does not yet exist. Bush and Mayer (1974: 402) wrote,

Most theories of income distribution which appear in the modern economic literature assume *well defined and perfectly enforced rules concerning property rights* [emphasis added]. The neoclassical theory of marginal productivity implicitly assumes a postconstitutional state in which a completely effective and cost free enforcement mechanism against theft has been institutionalized. If this were not the case, the usual assumption of selfishness would imply that an individual's income is his marginal product adjusted by the income transferred to him or from him through theft.

Bush and Mayer (1974: 401) went on to show that efficiency requires "orderly anarchy" defined as a society in which "no effort is spent in stealing property from others." However, the authors admit that enforcement is a public good and involves the "age old problem of who will protect individuals from the enforcer once the enforcer is given the power to enforce" (1974: 411). Thus, while Bush and Mayer showed that *some* set of well-defined and enforced property rights are required for efficiency, they do not attempt to specify what those rights are, what other rights are needed, whether those rights are legal or moral, or the source of sufficient incentives to comply with the rules.

Dan Usher (1992: 77–89) also rigorously proved that under anarchy (i.e., in the absence of rules) rational egoists will not behave competitively. He wrote that "Full and uncontested security of property is an essential assumption in the proof of the optimality of the competitive economy" (1992: 4). Summarizing his view, he wrote,

The model of anarchy tells us something about the model of perfect competition, for example, by emphasizing the implications of alternative assumptions. From our point of view, the main assumption of the model of perfect competition is security of property, attained effortlessly and at no cost to the participants in the economy. There is no better way of pointing out the implications of that assumption than by designing a society where the only security is one's ability to defend what one has from predators and where the process of taking and defending is costly and dangerous (Usher 1992: 98).

Usher did not show why strict rational egoists (i.e., individuals who interact completely unaffected by moral normative constraints) cannot achieve efficient outcomes of trade. Neither Bush and Mayer (1974) nor Usher (1992) have addressed the two other possible reasons for depicting agents as price-takers that have been advocated or implied by some accounts. Moreover, although both showed that enforced property rights are necessary for efficient outcomes of trade, others have argued that property rights can emerge spontaneously among a population of rational egoists. In Chapter 4, I show that strict rational egoists cannot enforce property rights and that property rights will not emerge spontaneously. Therefore, strict rational egoists cannot achieve Pareto-optimal allocations under trade. Finally, a set of well-defined and enforced property rights is not sufficient in itself to secure competitive behavior. Individuals behave competitively if and only if they are compelled by a system of moral normative constraints, which includes such property rights that are also "enforced" by a sufficient internal incentive to comply as well as other elements which I specify in Chapter 6.

In sum, three reasons jointly indicate why moral normative constraints are necessary conditions of competitive behavior. First, a presumption against non-market action entails a contradiction. This reason demonstrates that the conditions that secure competitive behavior must be identified and added as assumptions. Second, it is widely assumed that the common understanding of what constitutes a perfectly competitive market secures competitive behavior. But I show that given the common understanding of what constitutes a perfectly competitive market, some individuals will still have an incentive and the means to violate the rules of the process and will not behave competitively. Therefore, the common understanding of what constitutes a perfectly competitive market is not sufficient to achieve economically efficient allocations of commodities. Thus, some conditions are still missing and must be identified and added as background assumptions of the First Welfare Theorem. Finally, even if we alter assumptions (p_5) and (p_6)[1] so that agents have maximal information-processing capabilities and perfect information regarding every economically relevant variable, there exists the possibility that agents will not be able to decide what to do (more technically: there still exists a set of decision functions that are not effectively computable). So we shall see that more information is neither necessary nor sufficient for efficient outcomes of trade for strict rational egoists.

No other assumption can be altered so as to ensure competitive behavior, except to add moral normative constraints to the assumption set. I then show that, by adding moral normative constraints to the other assumptions, economically efficient outcomes of trade are achieved. It follows that moral normative constraints are necessary for Pareto-optimal equilibrium allocations of commodities achieved through market interaction.

Alternative Explanations for Price-Taking Behavior

Even though the proof of the First Welfare Theorem depends on competitive behavior, the context in which the proof is nested portrays every individual as taking any feasible action she believes will best maximize her own utility. If an agent is depicted as acting competitively for reasons other than the effects of moral normative constraints, then we must consider and discredit the rationale for these alternative reasons before we can conclude that moral normative constraints are necessary conditions of economic efficiency.

Although the notion of price-taking behavior (i.e., competitive behavior) is clear, its use among scholars is not univocal. Actions depend partially upon beliefs, and, given the ambiguous usage of the term *price-taking,* we are uncertain as to the beliefs on which price-taking behavior depends. In other words, when we say that agents act as price-takers, we must make clear whether such behavior depends on their beliefs regarding their potential effects on price levels or on their beliefs regarding alternative courses of action. For the purposes of clarifying the role of moral normative constraints, we have embedded a microeconomic model within a broader framework of situational analysis. Only by losing sight of the embeddedness of our analysis could we depict individuals as refraining from nonmarket actions when those actions promise efficiently to achieve individuals' desires.

Now then, why might strict rational egoists be depicted as price-takers under conditions of perfect competition? Why are they supposed to "behave competitively" if moral normative constraints are assumed not to exist? What factors in either the agent subset or the situation subset of assumptions that comprise our framework of situational analysis might account for competitive behavior? Given the derived principle of action (DPA), we know that individuals will act as price-takers only if each has good reason to believe that price-taking is the best feasible means to achieve σ_n. Since agents are strict rational egoists, hence no individual has a disposition to constrain utility-maximizing behavior. What then could be the "good reason" for refraining from non-market actions? Assumptions $(p_1)–(p_9)$ imply that we have only two alternatives: Either (1) we merely presume that each individual refrains from non-market action or (2) we assume that a perfectly competitive market as defined by assumption (p_6) is sufficient in itself to restrict agents' natural strategy domains. We will see that both of these assumptions are false, which means that we must alter the assumption set.

The Presumption against Nonmarket Action
Entails a Contradiction

Most, if not all, accounts of the First Welfare Theorem assume competitive behavior. When such proofs are set within Strict Rational Egoism, to merely assume competitive behavior is per force at least either to presume that agents choose only among alternative social states, not among alternative means to achieving their desired ends, or to assume that certain types of actions, which adversely affect the efficiency of outcomes, are never the best means for an agent to achieve his goals. However, recall that the instrumental rationality assumption presupposes a distinction between means and ends. Thus, by maintaining the integrity of the instrumental rationality assumption, we per force maintain a distinction between means and ends – between, that is, actions and their effects. When agents are depicted as choosing a most preferred social state without reference to why they choose to trade rather that to take some other action, the question of what means to adopt to achieve that social state does not come up. Therefore, in effect, assumption (p_8) – There are no moral rules – is rendered superfluous by the types of choices agents are pictured as taking. That is, even though we assume that each player may take any physically possible action, agents are represented in some accounts as choosing from among alternative consumption bundles that are ends, not means to ends. Thus, depicting agents choosing ends and not means to ends renders the absence of restrictions or the requirements on means provided by moral normative constraints irrelevant.

This consideration suggests that the theorem holds for Strict Rational Egoism because assumption (p_5) regarding instrumental rationality is overridden. But overriding the assumption of instrumental rationality, we either assume that no alternative means is available or imply a contradiction. Consider the first alternative. Since outcomes of market interaction will be efficient only if agents do not choose the best means to maximize utility, to override the instrumental rationality assumption is to assume that agents have no alternative means to chosen ends. But there is no justification for making such an assumption.

On the other hand, if some alternative means is more effective than trade and the instrumental rationality assumption is overridden by assuming that agents will not take that alternative means in the absence of moral normative constraints, then we face a contradiction. To show the contradiction, I must first clarify one implicit concept. Recall that assumption (p_1) indicates that individuals' preferences range over alternative social states defined only by alternative consumption bundles. Assumption (p_1) implies that preferences do not range over alternative visions of society as a whole, character types, or decision rules. It also implies that preferences do not range over others' attitudes or the relative satisfaction of others' goals, or even over any other types of considerations which I may have missed. A concise way to express this implication of assumption (p_1) is to say that each agents' preference relations are independent. Here are two arguments showing the contradiction:

(1) Assume that moral normative constraints are absent.
(2) Let agents be rational utility-maximizers having independent preference relations, which implies that they will always choose the most efficient means to maximize utility.
(3) There can be instances when using nonmarket behavior is the best means to maximize utility.
(4) Suppose agents do not resort to nonmarket behavior when doing so is the best means to maximize utility.
(5) Hence, agents do not choose the best means to maximize utility.
(6) Thus, agents are not rational utility-maximizers.
(7) (6) contradicts (2).

(1) Let agents be rational utility-maximizers having independent preference relations.
(2) Suppose agents do not resort to nonmarket behavior.
(3) Assume that moral normative constraints are absent.
(4) Agents do not resort to nonmarket behavior only if (a) there is some external norm and sanction that would constrain them from engaging in such behavior or (b) they have interdependent preference relations.
(5) Hence, either (a) there is some external norm and sanction that would constrain them from engaging in such behavior or (b) they have interdependent preference relations.
(6) (5a) contradicts (3) and (5b) contradicts (1).

Therefore, the presumption against nonmarket action is false; hence, agents choose from alternative means to desired ends, and some of those means may be nonmarket actions.

Perfectly Competitive Markets Cannot Ensure Competitive Behavior

In this section, we examine the second of three reasons why moral normative constraints are necessary conditions of competitive behavior. We just saw that a presumption against nonmarket action entails a contradiction. Now I will show that, under a widely accepted conception of a "perfectly competitive market," some individuals will have both an incentive and the means to violate the rules of the process. Therefore, given DPA, some agents will not behave competitively.

As a matter of definition, price-taking results from the belief that no individual's actions can affect the price of a commodity. It is generally held that numerous market participants, homogeneous products, freedom of exit and entry, and perfect information generate such a belief. These four components constitute the widely accepted idea of a perfectly competitive market. In the conclusion to this chapter, we offer an alternative account of a perfectly competitive market. Meanwhile, I argue that this account of a perfectly competitive market without moral normative constraints cannot ensure competitive behavior. Recall that the instrumental rationality assumption presupposes a distinction between means and ends (i.e., between actions and their effects). Microeconomic analysis presupposes a theory of behavior in which this distinction is essential. Therefore, by insisting on the distinction, we are doing nothing more than maintaining consistency in our analysis.

There is another reason to maintain a distinction between actions and their effects. The concept of an externality presupposes that a distinction exists between actions and their effects. An *externality* is the effect of some action related to production or consumption, which imposes an involuntary cost or benefit on some other agent and for which no compensation is made. External effects may be intended or unintended. Both types must be either precluded or, if not, at least rectified to achieve efficient outcomes. We will return to the concept of an externality and to this distinction between intended and unintended consequences later. For now, we assume that externalities are absent.

It is crucial that alternative actions, which are alternative means to outcomes, be adequately modeled, if an extended version of the theorem is accurately to depict the role of moral normative constraints and if failures to achieve efficient allocations of commodities are to be diagnosed correctly.

The fact that both the instrumental rationality assumption and the concept of an externality require a distinction between actions and their effects has one important consequence. Recall that we are using the broadest possible framework for analyzing social situations in that it takes into account all relevant features. Since the actions of other actors can result in social states that are not Pareto optimal, individuals must factor into their choices predictions about the choices of others. That is, they must estimate what others will do by reconstructing their probable reasoning. Individuals, therefore, act under strategic conditions.

Now, keeping in mind the strategic nature of the situation, we can phrase the issue at hand here as the following question:

(**Q**) *Is condition $(p_6)^2$ sufficient to eliminate every alternative action except price-taking?*

Assumption (p_6) expresses a widely accepted version of a perfectly competitive market. Our question, in other words, is this:

(**Q′**) *Does a perfectly competitive market without moral normative constraints ensure competitive behavior?*

We must refine our question to render it sufficiently precise. The one set of conventions for equilibrating supply and demand is a Walrasian auctioneer. A *Walrasian auctioneer* is an idealized agent who, upon receiving information regarding each individual's willingness to trade at a given price-ratio, adjusts prices until the total quantity supplied equals the total quantity demanded. (The process by which supply is equilibrated with demand is called the *tâtonnement*.) We want to determine whether the aspects of the common understanding of a perfectly competitive market are sufficient to ensure that agents respond only and truthfully to the price conventions. In other words,

(Q*) *Are the conditions expressed by assumption* (p_6) *sufficient to ensure that agents respond only and truthfully to the Walrasian auctioneer?*

Notice that assumption (p_8) – There are no moral rules – leaves open the possibility that agents may choose not to trade at all. To answer (Q*) in the negative, we must show that individuals have both an incentive not to respond truthfully and a means to carry out the deception. Once these two conditions are met, (DPA) indicates that agents will not act as price-takers.

The "numerous participants" requirement of this definition of a perfectly competitive market allows for noncompetitive behavior. Hurwicz (1972) showed that in economic environments with numerous, yet finitely many participants, there is no allocation mechanism having a no-trade option that is incentive compatible. Even though our situation and our agents constitute an economic environment that differs in significant respects from the environments Hurwicz specified,[3] his proof also holds in economic environments defined by assumptions (p_1)–(p_8). Hurwicz defined an *allocation mechanism* in terms of a game-form,[4] but we may describe his theorem informally. Hurwicz (1972: 320) characterized an allocation mechanism as being incentive compatible just in case no individual has an incentive to violate the rules of the process. Even in economic environments with a no-trade option such that the only permissible actions are to trade or to refrain from trading, Hurwicz showed that individuals have an incentive to misrepresent their willingness to pay to control prices. An individual can accomplish this by calculating a false offer curve (which is a false demand curve) such that, when combined with others' offer curves, it yields that equilibrium price-ratio that would have resulted if the individual had been a monopsonist, that is, if he had the direct control of a single buyer.

Let me explain this mechanism less formally. Recall that individuals are supposed to take prices as they are announced by a Walrasian auctioneer. Each trader then, on the basis of his preferences, determines what amount of each commodity he is willing to buy or sell at those prices and reports the results to the auctioneer. Unless all commodities that agents desire to sell are sold and all that agents desire to buy are acquired, the auctioneer calls out a revised set of prices – lowering (raising) the exchange ratio on those unsold commodities

(commodities not offered for sale). Thus, an allocation mechanism such as the Walrasian auctioneer receives information from individuals and then computes a feasible allocation. Whenever an equilibrium is reached, each participant is allocated his stated demand. However, an agent can receive more than his true demand by misreporting it. Suppose that there are two commodities and an agent falsely reports that he would like four units of each based on his current endowment. He then calculates a set of preferences that corresponds to his false offer and acts accordingly [i.e., suppose that, to be consistent, he pretends to be indifferent with respect to these alternatives (10,1), (8,2), (6,3), (4,4), (3,5), (2,7), (1,10)]. Therefore, at any alternative price-ratio, he makes it appear as though he is price-taking when, in fact, he is misrepresenting his true demand. The resulting equilibrium allocation is not Pareto optimal. Since this strategy best achieves what that individual desires, he will take it. Therefore, Hurwicz' impossibility theorem combined with (DPA) entails the denial of (Q*), that is, that the conditions expressed by assumption (p_6) are not sufficient to ensure that agents respond only and truthfully to the Walrasian auctioneer. Moral normative constraints are part of a set of normative conditions that are individually necessary and jointly sufficient.

Maximal Information-Processing Capabilities and Perfect Information Are Not Sufficient for Pareto-Optimal Equilibrium Allocations

In Chapter 2, we saw that, even though the proof of the First Welfare Theorem depends on competitive behavior, Strict Rational Egoism (the situation against which the assumptions of the proof are compared) portrays every individual as taking any feasible action she believes will best maximize her own utility. In other words, there is no reason to think that the competitive behavior required by the First Welfare Theorem will be secured in Strict Rational Egoism. If an agent is depicted as acting competitively for reasons other than the effects of moral normative constraints, then we must consider and undermine the rationale for these alternative reasons before we can conclude that moral normative constraints are necessary conditions of economic efficiency.

Social situations defined by assumptions (p_1)–(p_9) permit only two possible explanations for portraying strict rational egoists as price-takers under conditions of perfect competition: either (1) we presume that for no sufficient reason each individual simply refrains from nonmarket action, or (2) we assume that a perfectly competitive market as defined by assumption (p_6)[5] restricts agents' natural strategy domains. In the first case, the depiction is contrary both to the instrumental rationality assumption and to the Derived Principle for Action and leads to a contradiction. The second explanation is ruled out because Hurwicz's (1972) impossibility proof applies to a perfectly competitive market defined by assumption (p_6). Agents, therefore, have both an incentive to misrepresent their true demand and the means to carry it out. However, the "perfect information" component of assumption (p_6) indicates that individuals have perfect information regarding every economically relevant variable, except with respect to the preference relations and the natural strategy domains of others. The perfect information component of assumption (p_6) is not empirically implausible. However, theoretically speaking, the perfect information component of assumption (p_6) could be extended to others' preference relations and natural strategy domains. It could then be claimed that if agents possess maximal information-processing capabilities and perfect information regarding every economically relevant variable, nonmarket actions will be precluded and equilibrium allocations will be Pareto optimal because every agent will know that everyone is able to anticipate and to neutralize noncompetitive behavior and that every agent also knows that everyone else knows this. If so, then in theory moral normative constraints would not be necessary. All that is needed is better information. In other words, an objection based on such an extension of the perfect information component of assumption (p_6) could be raised against the Moral Thesis. Therefore, to establish that moral normative constraints are necessary conditions of efficient outcomes of trade, I must respond to this question: If agents have maximal information-processing capabilities, is perfect information sufficient for Pareto-optimal equilibrium allocations? Stated in more detail, the question is this:

In social situations defined by assumptions (p_1)–(p_9), *if agents have maximal information-processing capabilities, is perfect information regarding every economically relevant variable in a context that requires simultaneous, rather than sequential[6] decisions, in conjunction with the other conditions cited in assumption* (p_6), *sufficient to ensure price-taking behavior and, therefore, sufficient to achieve Pareto-optimal equilibrium allocations?*

Informally speaking, if it can be shown that, in social situations defined by assumptions (p_1)–(p_9) (where perfect information is thus extended) there exists the possibility that agents will not be able to decide what to do, then perfect information is not sufficient to secure competitive behavior, and the objection is, therefore, refuted. Moreover, it will also follow that no information-revealing mechanism for strict rational egoism can rectify the result. Only a set of moral normative constraints will make Pareto-optimal equilibrium allocations possible for strict rational egoists – even in the theoretical ideal.[7] In the pages that follow, I offer such an argument. This, then is the third reason why moral normative constraints are necessary conditions of efficient outcomes of market interaction:

Even if we alter assumptions (p_5) and (p_6) so that agents have maximal information-processing capabilities and perfect information regarding every economically relevant variable, there exists the possibility that no agent will be able to decide what to do.

Perfect Information and Full Rationality

By the term *perfect information,* I mean complete and symmetrically distributed information regarding every economically relevant variable. That is to say, each individual is aware of the complete social situation in which he finds himself; no factor of the situation that could affect any individual's utility level is hidden. Stated in the formal terms we have adopted, we say that each agent knows each economically relevant variable pertinent to every other agent including every element of the entire social situation.[8] Because perfect information covers every economically relevant variable, it entails common knowledge. That is, each agent knows that every other agent knows the complete social situation including the fact that everyone knows that everyone knows, and so on. To gather all these diverse elements together in one concise statement of three broad categories of knowledge, we say that each agent knows (1) every relevant characteristic regarding every *agent* including, of course, himself; (2) the value of every relevant variable in the *situation;* (3) that every other individual knows (1) and (2); and (4) that everyone knows (3). In what follows, I develop these ideas in stages and formalize them to provide a rigorous and clear statement of the problem.

We can represent the information-processing capability of each agent as an abstract computer that "remembers" sets and relations, and that is programmed to enumerate any effectively enumerable set or relation and to compute any effectively computable function. Informally, we say that a function is *effectively computable* if and only if there is an algorithm such that when given any element from the domain of the function as input, the algorithm gives as its output the unique element from the range of the function. Accordingly, we approach the central question before us using some concepts and established results in computability theory. Two established results are crucial to this question. First of all, I suppose that individuals' information-processing capabilities are Universal Turing Machines. A *Universal Turing Machine* is an abstract computer in which the limitations attached to actual computers (e.g., time, speed, and material) are irrelevant, and which can compute every effectively computable function.[9] Imagine it this way: In every respect, individuals' cognitive capacities are those of a normal human being, except that each can store information and compute functions better than normal human beings. But individuals in our model differ from computers and are similar to humans in that each is capable of second-order awareness; they are aware *that* they are perceiving, computing, desiring, and the like. In computability theory, a second standard result, which is integral to our argument, is that the class of effectively computable functions is coextensive with the class of Turing-computable functions.[10] Therefore, for any function f, individuals in our model can (cannot) compute f, if f is (is not) effectively computable.[11]

The particular course of action an individual takes, therefore, is a matter of that individual's computing a function. Let a *decision function* be the function that each individual computes to be able to decide what action to take. The elements of each individual's decision function is specified, given the factors of information individuals have in their possession. I will show that there exists the possibility that no agent will be able to decide what to do. I will accomplish this by showing that there exists a set of decision functions that is not effectively computable.

Information Units

We have before us four broad categories[12] regarding which individuals possess perfect information. To describe adequately the members of these categories and how they affect individuals' decisions, we must relate these categories of individuals' knowledge to the analytical framework within which we are working and to the premises of the First Welfare Theorem. Recall that we are now treating assumptions (p_1)–(p_9) as the assumptions of the version of the First Welfare Theore we examined in Chapter 2. Recall also that assumptions (p_1)–(p_9) instantiate the analytical elements of the social situation which is divided into two categories – the agent subset and the situation subset. Since every agent possesses perfect information regarding each element in both subsets, each individual is fully aware of each one of assumptions (p_1)–(p_9) – not as an element in an analytical model of social interaction nor as a premise in a proof but as a feature of the situation in which they act.

Viewed as features of the situation in which they act, every element of the agent category or the situation category varies in its instantiation with respect to each individual, thereby contributing to the difference that exists between different individuals' decision-pertinent data. For example, assumption (p_7) is Agents control finite resources. But from the perspective of each individual, even though each individual faces the fact that each individual controls finite resources, each individual set of resources varies in its content. Seven such elements or factors from the agent category and the situation category are directly pertinent to each individual's decision.

Factor 1. Everyone knows that every individual is fully rational in that each is maximally capable of storing and processing information.

Factor 2. Every individual knows the set of all individuals in the action arena.

Factor 3. Everyone knows the set of strategies feasible for every individual.

Factor 4. Everyone knows the set of combinations of all strategies.

Factor 5. Each individual knows the set of potential outcomes achieved by alternative combinations of strategies.

Factor 6. Every agent knows every individual's utility function defined on the set of potential outcomes.

Factor 7. Every individual knows factors (1) through (6) and that everyone knows factor (7), that is, that everyone knows that everyone knows.

We can then provide detail to each of these factors to picture more easily the decision process of strict rational egoists.

FACTOR 1. Everyone knows that every individual is fully rational in that each is maximally capable of storing and processing information. Therefore, each individual must take into consideration and calculate every other individual's decision functions because the situation is strategic and noncooperative.

FACTOR 2. Every individual knows the set of all individuals in the action arena. This element means that every individual has a list containing the names of all individuals, can determine how many individuals are on the list, and can pick out any individual from the list. Let the set of individual's names be denoted by $I = \{1, \ldots, n\}$. Each individual i has a complete list of each $i \in I$ in his memory, as follows: Each $i \in I$ is assigned exactly one positive integer beginning with the positive integer 1. No two individuals are assigned the same integer. Thus, $I = \{1, \ldots, n\} \subseteq \mathbb{N}$. Let $max(I)$ be the effectively computable function that gives the maximum value of I. Let $f_I : \mathbb{N} \to \mathbb{N}$ be the effectively computable function that associates exactly one positive integer with a name of an individual; no two individuals have the same name.[13]

Thus, every individual knows how many agents are in I because he can compute $max(I)$, and every individual i can identify (i.e., pick out) any $i \in I$, $i = 1, \ldots, n$, because he can compute f_I.

FACTOR 3. Everyone knows the set of strategies feasible for every other individual. In other words, every individual i knows the set of strategies feasible for each $i \in I$, which we call i's *natural strategy domain*, and denote as S^i. This means that, for each S^i, every individual has a list containing the index numbers of each strategy in S^i, knows how many strategies are on each list, and can pick out any strategy from any list. For the sake of simplicity without loss of generality, we define a *strategy* a_n^i as the nth single course of action available to individual i under a particular set of conditions.[14] Each individual has a complete list of each $a_n^i \in S^i$ in her memory, as follows: Each $a_n^i \in S^i$ is assigned exactly one positive integer beginning with a_n^i, and no two strategies are assigned the same integer. Hence, for each individual i, $S^i = \{a_n^1, \ldots, a_n^i\}$, where each n is its index number. Let $max(S^i)$ be the effectively computable function that gives the maximum index number in S^i. Let $f_S^i : k \to S^i$, for $k = \{1, \ldots, n\}$, be the effectively computable function that associates a single positive integer with each $a_n^i \in S^i$.

Thus, every individual knows how many strategies are in S^i because he can compute $\max(S^i)$, and each individual can identify any $a_n^i \in S^i$ because he can compute f_S^i. Each individual knows the class $K = \{S^1, \ldots, S^n\}$ of all natural strategy domains S^i, $i = 1, \ldots n$. Each individual holds in memory a complete list of each $S^n \in K$, such that exactly one positive integer is assigned to each strategy domain beginning with S^1, until the list $S^1, \ldots, S^n$, is complete, and no two natural strategy domains are assigned the same integer. Furthermore, each individual knows how many natural strategy domains S^i are on the list and can pick out any strategy domain from the list K or any strategy from any natural strategy domain. Let the effectively computable function $f_K : k \rightarrow K$, for $k = \{1, \ldots, n\}$, be the function that associates a single positive integer with each $S^i \in K$. Therefore, each individual can identify any $S^i \in K$ because he can compute f_K, and each individual knows how many are on the list because he knows how many individuals there are and their "names."

FACTOR 4. Everyone knows the set of combinations of all strategies. Let $SX = \{s_1, \ldots, s_n\}$ be the Cartesian product of the S^is, where each s_n represents one strategy n-tuple in SX. Let $h: SX \rightarrow Z$ represent the effectively computable outcome function, where Z is the outcome space. In other words, h maps each total combination of actions, $s_n \in SX$, into the outcome space Z. Each individual knows the unique social state achieved by any $s_n \in SX$ only if he knows SX and he can compute h. This means that every individual has a list containing the index number of all $s_n \in SX$, knows how many social states are on the list, and can pick out any social state from the list. Each individual has a complete list of each $s_n \in SX$ in his memory, as follows: each $s_n \in SX$ is assigned exactly one positive integer beginning with s_1, and no two collective strategies are assigned the same integer. SX is effectively enumerable. Let the effectively computable function $f_{SX} : k \rightarrow K$, for $k = \{1, \ldots, n\}$, be the function that associates a single positive integer with each $s_n \in SX$. Let the effectively computable function $h : SX \rightarrow Z$ map the set of strategy n-tuples onto the set of outcomes. The function h is a *one-to-one onto* function. The function h is one-to-one because $\forall s_n, s_m \in \mathrm{dom}(h), s_n \neq s_m \Rightarrow h(s_n) \neq h(s_m)$, and onto because $\mathrm{dom}(h) = SX$ and $\mathrm{ran}(h) = Z$.

Each individual can compute the Cartesian product of two sets, given correct information regarding the elements of each set. In this case, each individual knows how many individuals there are and how many actions are available to each. Given this fact, we observe that each individual can pick out any strategy n-tuple because he can compute f_{SX}. Furthermore, because each individual can compute the function h for each action $s_n \in SX$, every agent knows the social state σ_n for which s_n is necessary and sufficient. But he must be able to determine $a_n^i \in s_n$, which indicates his own part in achieving the σ_n associated with s_n. Let $g_n^i: s_n \rightarrow a_n^i$ represent the effectively computable function that picks out i's action in the collective strategy s_n. There are, of course, several such functions: one for each s_n.

FACTOR 5. Each individual knows the set of potential outcomes achieved by alternative combinations of strategies. *Potential outcomes* is referred to alternatively as *social states*. This means that every individual has a list containing the names of all social states, knows how many names of social states are on the list, and can pick out any social state from the list. Social states are defined by alternative allocations of commodities. Let the set of names of possible social states be denoted by $Z = \{\sigma_1, \ldots, \sigma_n\}$, where each n is its index number. Each individual has a complete list of each $\sigma_n \in Z$ in her memory, as follows: each $\sigma_n \in Z$ is assigned exactly one positive integer beginning with σ_1, and no two social states are assigned the same integer. Let max(Z) be the effectively computable function that gives the maximum value of Z. Let $f_Z : k \to Z$, for $k = \{1, \ldots, n\}$, be the effectively computable function that associates a single positive integer with each $\sigma_n \in Z$.

Thus, every individual knows how many social states are in Z because she can compute max(Z), and each individual can identify any $\sigma_n \in Z$ because she can compute f_Z.

FACTOR 6. Every agent knows every individual's utility function defined on the set of potential outcomes, Z. For the sake of clarity of presentation, we first show that each individual knows his or her own utility function. Technically speaking, a utility function $u(x)$ assigns a numerical value to each member of a set X of alternatives. For our purposes, X is a set of alternative social states.

We begin with the supposition that each agent knows his or her own preference relation on Z. Notice that Z is not a set of alternative consumption bundles but rather a set of alternative social states characterized in part by alternative consumption bundles. Stipulating that the symbol $\succcurlyeq_i^Z$ represents individual i's preference relation on Z, we assume, as we did in Chapter 2, that $\succcurlyeq_i^Z$ is reflexive, transitive, complete, and continuous.

Every preference relation having these four properties can be represented as a utility function.[15] Let $U_i : Z \to B \subseteq \mathbb{R}$, for all i, where $\mathbb{R}$ is the set of real numbers, and B is a proper subset of $\mathbb{R}$, represent an effectively computable individual utility function. We want to indicate that for any two social states, individual i thinks that the first is as least as good as the second if and only if the utility value of the first is greater than or equal to the second. Hence, each U_i: $Z \to B \subseteq \mathbb{R}$ is a utility function such that

$$\forall \, \sigma_m, \sigma_n \in Z \, [\sigma_m \succcurlyeq_i \sigma_n \Leftrightarrow U_i(\sigma_m) \geq U_i(\sigma_m)]$$

Let u_m^i be a real number representing the value i's utility function U_i, for some argument, σ_m, that is, $U_i(\sigma_m) = u_m^i$. Each $u_m^i \in \text{ran}(U_i)$, that is, each $u_m^i \in B \subseteq \mathbb{R}$ can be given an ordinal ranking, beginning with the integer 1. Let the effectively computable function $f_B : B \to A \subseteq \mathbb{N}$ be a one-to-one onto function whose domain $= \mathrm{ran}(U_i)$ and whose range $= \{1, \ldots, n\}$, such that

$$\forall\, u^i_m, u^i_n \in B, \qquad \forall\, n,m \in A\ [u^i_m > u^i_n \Leftrightarrow n > m]$$

Hence, $f_B(u^i_m) = n$. Let the function $f_A : A \subseteq \mathbb{N} \to Z$ be a one-to-one onto function whose domain $= \mathrm{ran}(f_B)$, and whose range $= Z$. Hence, $f_A(n) = \sigma_n$.

Note that each function U_i is a one-to-one onto function. U_i is one-to-one because $\forall x,y \in \mathrm{dom}(U_i)$, $x \neq y \Rightarrow U_i(x) \neq U_i(y)$, and U_i is onto because $\mathrm{dom}(U_i) = Z$, and $\mathrm{ran}(U_i) = B$.

For each outcome $\sigma_n \in Z$, each individual i knows its ordinal rank of n possible alternatives for each $i \in I$ because i can compute each U_i, f_B, and f_A.

FACTOR 7. Every individual knows factors 1 through 6, and that everyone knows factor 7, that is, that everyone knows that everyone knows. At the risk of redundancy, we state the same idea in other words: Each agent knows (1) that everyone knows that every individual is a utility-maximizing, instrumentally rational, Turing-machine calculator; (2) that every individual has a list containing the names of all individuals, knows how many individuals are on the list, and can pick out any individual from the list; (3) that every individual has a list containing the index number of all social states, knows how many social states are on the list, and can pick out any social state from the list; (4) that everyone knows everyone's utility function; (5) that everyone knows everyone's feasible actions; (6) that everyone knows the outcomes that follow from those actions; and (7) that everyone knows that everyone knows (1) through (6).

Parametric Choice

For each strategy n-tuple, $s_n \in SX$, there exists a social state σ_n for which s_n is both necessary and sufficient, while $a^i_n \in s_n$ is only necessary. But where, for some individual i, the actions of agents other than i are irrelevant, a^i_n is both necessary and sufficient to achieve σ_n. Let a *parametric decision function* be a type of decision function in which common knowledge is not a factor and in which the actions of other agents are irrelevant.[16] Hence, where other individuals' actions are irrelevant, an agent maximizes utility if and only if she takes that action a^i_n which achieves that social state holding the highest level of utility. In other words, the particular decision that an individual makes (i.e., the strategy that she pursues) is the one that maximizes utility. Therefore, to decide what action to take, each individual must make the following determinations. First of all, an individual must determine what social state gives the highest level of utility, u^i. Recall that each $U_i: Z \to B \subseteq \mathbb{R}$. Each agent, thus, must ascertain the highest value in *B*. Let the effectively computable function, max(B_i), pick out the highest value in *B*.

By computing max(B_i), f_B, and f_A, each agent can determine what social state gives her the highest level of utility. Second, each individual must determine what collective strategy achieves that outcome by computing h^{-1}. Finally, each agent must determine what individual action is a member of that collective strategy by computing g_n^i. Therefore, we represent *i*'s decision as the value of her parametric decision function as follows:

$$a_n^i = g_n^i(h^{-1}(f_A(f_B(\max(B_i)))))$$

Proposition. *Every parametric decision function $g_n^i(h^{-1}(f_A(f_B(\max(B_i)))))$ is effectively computable.*

Notice that the first step in a decision process is finding the social state with the highest ordinal value. Perhaps an explanation for this claim is in order. Some types of relevant data (some of which are given and others of which require calculation or experimentation) are not directly relevant to the argument of this chapter. To depict how agents acquire these types of information would needlessly complicate things. So, examples include a list of all individuals and a list of strategies for each individual. Only that each agent knows the set of all agents and all their actions is relevant to our argument. Calculating the Cartesian product of all strategy domains is not relevant to the proof. Neither is the manner in which the set of possible outcomes is determined. We only require a mapping of strategy *n*-tuples onto outcomes having alternative payoffs. Therefore, we simply assume a finite set of outcomes. Finally, each preference relation on the set of outcomes is given, and calculating each utility function from its corresponding preference relation is not relevant. With this much information at their disposal, the next step individuals take is to find the outcome yielding the highest utility. This step is the first step in the process of computing a decision function.

Quasiparametric Decision. Let a *quasiparametric decision* be one in which some, but not all, of every other agent's actions in a strategy *n*-tuple are irrelevant. We will refer to such types of decisions later. We bring it up now because of its relation to both parametric and strategic choice.

Conditional Decision. Let a *conditional decision* be a stage in a decision process in which an individual must consider a range of hypothetical alternatives before making a final decision. Each hypothetical alternative is a conditional decision. Each agent reasons in this manner: Suppose I take action a_n^i, and *j* takes action $a_{n'}^j$, and so on, social state σ_n will follow. The kinds of parametric decisions with which we are concerned do not involve conditional decisions in this sense simply because alternative means are incorporated into the set of social states so that, by choosing the social state having the highest ordinal value, an individual chooses both a goal and the best means to achieve it.

Strategic Choice

For each individual i, the action i takes depends on the maximum value of his utility function, which itself depends in part on the actions taken by every other agent to achieve the maximum value of their respective utility functions. Hence, each individual must take others' decision functions into account. Therefore, strategic decisions involve conditional decisions because individuals first compute a parametric decision function and then determine which *other* strategy n-tuples of which the action a_n^i is a member. Each strategy n-tuple, except one, results in a social state different than the one that gives the calculating agent her highest utility. We give a summary version of each individual's decision function as follows:

$$a_n^i = g_n^i(s_m : g_n^i(h^{-1}(f_A(f_B(\max(B_i))))) = g_n^j(h^{-1}(f_A(f_B(\max(B_j))))),$$
$$\forall j \neq i)$$

Decision functions are effectively computable if and only if there exists a Nash equilibrium of strategies, that is, given every other players' strategy, no other strategy yields a higher payoff. Thus, the effective computability of decision functions depends on the character of each utility function. Our concern now is to show that there exists a set of decision functions that is not effectively computable.

There Exists a Set of Utility Functions That Render These Decision Functions Not Effectively Computable under Conditions of Perfect Information

An alternative way to state the proposition is that there is a set of utility functions for which there is no Nash equilibrium of strategies so that no individual's decision function is effectively computable. Suppose that the Walrasian auctioneer presents each individual i with an initial price vector p^*. Each individual's natural strategy domain includes three possible alternative actions: defraud by overstatement, trade, or defraud by understatement. That is, for each individual i, $S^i = \{a_1^i, a_2^i, a_3^i\}$, where $a_1^i = +\text{fraud}$, $a_2^i = \text{trade}$, and $a_3^i = -\text{fraud}$. Each individual then computes a decision function to give him the best course of action. Finally, each agent simultaneously presents his trading decision to the Walrasian auctioneer, where a trading decision is a list of the amount of each commodity the agent presents himself as willing to trade, given p^*. We present the case for two individuals which can be extended to n individuals without loss of generality.

Now, before I present the specifics of the proof and to make the proof itself more perspicuous, I will present and respond to a possible objection that perfect information seems to rule out the possibility of fraud. The objection could be argued as follows:

> The proof requires that agents' natural strategy domains include two means to defraud. But since the perfect information assumption has been strengthened so as to include common knowledge of every agent's utility function defined over possible outcomes, the possibility of fraud by overstatement or understatement of one's preferences to the Walrasian auctioneer is ruled out. That is, to defraud by either of these means involves stating one's preferences to be what everyone knows them not to be. Thus, fraud is not an alternative to trade as the proof seems to require.

We must keep in mind the difference between *possible actions,* which are members of an agent's *natural* strategy domain, and *effective actions,* which are members of agent's *rational* strategy domain, which is a subset of that agent's natural strategy domain. The fact that each agent knows every other agents' utility function does not render the actions impossible. It only renders them ineffective. Fraud by overstatement or understatement of one's preferences to the Walrasian auctioneer remains a possible action and, therefore, a member of the agent's natural strategy domain. Perfect information is supposed to render such possible actions ineffective, thus ruling out non-price-taking behavior and leaving trade as the only option. Indeed, in principle, for some or even most sets of utility functions defined over outcomes, perfect information in this framework will eliminate non-price-taking behavior, thus rendering it sufficient for efficient outcomes without moral normative constraints. However, as the forthcoming proof shows, for this given set of utility functions, even though agents know each other's utility functions, they cannot come to a decision regarding which action to take. Part of each agent's decision process involves first identifying the most preferred outcome and the action that is supposed to achieve that outcome. Then, realizing that everyone else knows his most preferred outcome and its means and that they can respond in such a way as to take advantage of such a move, the agent considers an alternative. But others know this as well. Each agent knows this about every other agent. They cannot, given this particular set of decision functions, achieve that efficient outcome, which results when both decide to trade. Thus, perfect information regarding every economically relevant variable and perfect information-processing capabilities are not sufficient to achieve economic efficiency. However, the addition of moral

Table 3. *A Possible Two-Agent Situation*

	a_1^2, +fraud	a_2^2, trade	a_3^2, -fraud
a_1^1, + fraud	16,8	9,2	4,14
a_2^1, trade	13,10	6,12	10,6
a_3^1, -fraud	7,18	8,1	12,3

normative constraints to that same social situation ensures economic efficiency by ruling out fraud.

Consider now the specifics of the proof. In Table 3, I list the natural strategy domains, $S^i = \{a_1^i, a_2^i, a_3^i\}$ for each individual i, and the payoff each individual receives for each action a_n^i. Some of the information that each agent possesses is given here:

1. $I = \{1, 2\}$;
2. $Z = \{\sigma_1, \ldots, \sigma_9\}$;
3. $U_1 = \{\langle\sigma_1, 9\rangle, \langle\sigma_2, 5\rangle, \langle\sigma_3, 1\rangle, \langle\sigma_4, 8\rangle, \langle\sigma_5, 2\rangle, \langle\sigma_6, 6\rangle, \langle\sigma_7, 3\rangle, \langle\sigma_8, 4\rangle, \langle\sigma_9, 7\rangle\}$, and
   $U_2 = \{\langle\sigma_1, 5\rangle, \langle\sigma_2, 2\rangle, \langle\sigma_3, 8\rangle, \langle\sigma_4, 6\rangle, \langle\sigma_5, 7\rangle, \langle\sigma_6, 4\rangle, \langle\sigma_7, 9\rangle, \langle\sigma_8, 1\rangle, \langle\sigma_9, 3\rangle\}$;
4. $K = \{S^1, S^2\}$, where $S^1 = \{a_1^1, a_2^1, a_3^1\}$, and $S^2 = \{a_1^2, a_2^2, a_3^2\}$;
5. $SX = \{\langle a_1^1, a_1^2\rangle, \langle a_1^1, a_2^2\rangle, \langle a_1^1, a_3^2\rangle, \langle a_2^1, a_1^2\rangle, \langle a_2^1, a_2^2\rangle, \langle a_2^1, a_3^2\rangle, \langle a_3^1, a_1^2\rangle, \langle a_3^1, a_2^2\rangle, \langle a_3^1, a_3^2\rangle\}$,
   where $s_1 = \langle a_1^1, a_1^2\rangle$, $s_2 = \langle a_1^1, a_2^2\rangle, \ldots, s_9 = \langle a_3^1, a_3^2\rangle$;
6. $h = \{\langle s_1, \sigma_1\rangle, \ldots, \langle s_9, \sigma_9\rangle\}$.

Each Individual's Strategic Decision Process

(In what follows, social states are named beginning with σ_1 at the top left and moving to the right.) In general, the first step in the process of computing a decision function is to find the outcome yielding the highest utility. Each agent then searches for the strategy n-tuple that achieves that social state yielding the highest level of utility for i and determines whether the strategy n-tuple that achieves it is a Nash equilibrium. According to factors 5 and 6, each individual knows the set of potential outcomes achieved by alternative combinations of strategies, and every agent knows every individual's utility function defined on the set of potential outcomes. Therefore, each individual begins by making a conditional decision that is aimed at determining what action yields the social state giving the highest level of utility and that, in turn, is achieved by computing the parametric decision function

$$a_n^i = g_n^i(h^{-1}(f_A(f_B(\max(B_i))))).$$

By computing $\max(B_i)$, f_B, and f_A, each agent can determine what social state gives him the highest level of utility. For individual 1 that state is σ_1 yielding a payoff value of 16. Individual 1 then must associate σ_1 with its corresponding strategy n-tuple by computing the inverse function $h^{-1}: Z \to SX$. The value of the function h^{-1} for σ_1 is s_1. Individual 1 determines his action in strategy n-tuple s_1 by computing the function g_1^1, which yields the output a_1^1.

Individual 1 will not conclude at this point that he should take action a_1^1. He must first determine how many strategy n-tuples involve the action a_1^1 and determine which action every other agent will take to achieve their highest payoff. Since for a set of individuals $I = \{1, \ldots, n\}$, there are m^n strategy k-tuples for each action $a_n^i \in S^i = \{a_1^i, \ldots, a_m^i\}$, there are $m \times n - 1$ strategy k-tuples in which a particular action of one individual is paired with i's action. Since, in this example, there are two individuals and for each individual j, $S^j = \{a_1^j, a_2^j, a_3^j\}$, individual 1 must, therefore, consider three different strategy k-tuples.

Individual 1 reasons as follows: Suppose I take action a_1^1. Then individual 2, knowing my utility function and so on, will not take action a_1^2 yielding a payoff of 8, but will take a_3^2 yielding a payoff of 14, knowing as I do that he is instrumentally rational and so on. But since I know that 2 knows what he knows, I should take action a_3^1. But if I take action a_3^1, then 2 will take action a_1^2. If 2 will take action a_1^2, then I will take action a_1^1.

Individual 1 has completed the first round of an infinite loop. Regardless of which action either agent begins with, each encounters a potentially infinite loop.

Given these utility functions, there is no social state s_m such that the value of the function, $h^{-1}(f_A(f_B(\max(B_i))))$, for some individual i equals the value of the function, $h^{-1}(f_A(fB(\max(B_j))))$, for every individual $j \neq i$. Therefore, no individual can compute his decision function. Hence, there exists a set of decision functions that are not effectively computable.

Perfect Information Is Not a Sufficient Condition for Pareto-Optimal Equilibrium Allocations

We began this chapter with the following question in mind:

If agents have maximal information-processing capabilities, is perfect information regarding every economically relevant variable in a context that requires simultaneous, rather than sequential, decisions in conjunction with the other conditions cited in assumption (p_6), sufficient to en-

sure price-taking behavior and, therefore, sufficient to achieve Pareto-optimal equilibrium allocations?

We conclude that since there exists a case in which no decision function is effectively computable, perfect information is not sufficient to secure price-taking behavior. It follows that perfect information is not sufficient to achieve Pareto-optimal outcomes. Agents are not themselves Turing Machines, they only possess Turing Machine computing capabilities. Since agents are capable of second-order awareness, if they discover a repeating loop in their computations, they will shut down until such time as new inputs change the structure of the situation.[17] Therefore, as we might expect, we can construct an allocation that consists of the set of initial endowments in social state s_0 and which yields a payoff vector, 6, 11. Had each agent taken the "trade" option, they would have achieved an equilibrium allocation under social state s_5 in which one of them would had been better off than in social state s_0, and none would have been worse off. Thus, social state s_5 is Pareto superior to social state s_0. In this economy, in which moral normative constraints are absent but all the conditions of standard accounts of a perfectly competitive market hold, the equilibrium allocation that individuals end up with is not Pareto optimal.

It may be objected that the result holds only in conjunction with the particular version of the Walrasian price mechanism presented here. In response, we claim that the result is not dependent on any particular price mechanism. The result holds even in the Arrow–Debreu model, where no action is taken until a message equilibrium is found. Given the utility functions described in the example, no message equilibrium is possible. Therefore, the result holds wherever agents must make simultaneous decisions. A model that involves simultaneous decisions is more realistic. Moreover, as long as agents must decide simultaneously, it is impossible to improve the situation with any type of information-revealing mechanism.

Moral Normative Constraints Are Necessary for Economically Efficient Outcomes of Market Interaction

Agents act as price-takers in versions of the First Welfare Theorem that specify moral normative constraints because moral normative constraints ensure that agents act competitively. That is, moral normative constraints must be among the background assumptions of the First Welfare Theorem.

To facilitate the discussion, it might help to see the logical form of our critique. Let $\{p_1 \& , \ldots , \& p_9\}$ symbolize the initial set of assumptions of the First Welfare Theorem in which agents are strict rational egoists and in which morality plays no role. Let $\forall x [EA_x \Rightarrow PO_x]$ symbolize the First Welfare Theorem itself – Every equilibrium allocation is Pareto optimal. Our critique of the idea of a perfectly competitive market without moral normative constraints has the following logical form. We have supposed (S1):

(S1) Suppose $\{p_1 \& , \ldots , \& p_9\} \Leftrightarrow \forall x \, [EA_x \Rightarrow PO_x]$

But then we have shown (S2), which is a denial of (S1):

(S2) But $\underline{\{p_1 \& , \ldots , \& p_9\} \Rightarrow \exists x \, [EA_x \& \neg PO_x]}$

We must conclude that the assumption set is not sufficient to achieve economically efficient outcomes of trade:

(S3) Thus, $\neg\{\{p_1 \& , \ldots , \& p_9\} \Rightarrow \forall x \, [EA_x \Rightarrow PO_x]\}$

It follows that if every equilibrium allocation of commodities achieved through market interaction is Pareto optimal, at least one assumption in the initial set must be false. We must show which assumptions are false and specify alternative assumptions that are both necessary and sufficient for Pareto-optimal equilibrium allocations of commodities achieved through trade.

Note that perfect information regarding every economically relevant variable is not itself a necessary condition. If we reduce the extent of perfect information, making it complete for some aspects of the action arena, but not for all, we have shown that agents will compute parametric decision functions, but reducing the extent of perfect information means that individuals' information will be asymmetrically distributed for some economically relevant variables. However, it is well known that asymmetric information makes force and fraud possible by creating the appropriate incentives. Therefore, for the First Welfare Theorem to hold in this economy when we eliminate (or restrict the range of) perfect information, we must also eliminate the incentives to take detrimental actions. Thus, perfect information regarding every economically relevant variable is neither sufficient nor necessary. I claim moral normative constraints are necessary and the assumption set that includes them is sufficient.

To make the case, I return once more to the question of why agents might act as price-takers. We now see that perfect information is not sufficient to secure price-taking behavior. If we can show in our model just how moral normative constraints can achieve what perfect information cannot, we will have demonstrated[18] that moral normative constraints are necessary conditions of the First Welfare Theorem. A moral normative constraint can be construed as a moral right coupled with an incentive to comply with its demands, thus effectively restricting the types of actions agents can take.[19] In principle, then, it is possible to convert this example into a model in which the First Welfare Theorem holds by introducing moral rights (which render the decision function quasiparametric in that some feasible actions by other agents that would have been required to be taken into consideration need not be now) and by altering the *Agents* subset to include a sufficient internal incentive to comply with all moral rights. Thus, in our example, we remove actions a_1^i and a_3^i for each individual i by introducing a moral right to true information and a sufficient internal incentive to comply. Each agent's decision function is then computable, and each agent decides to trade.[20]

Since we have shown that strict rational egoists will not comply with any enforcement mechanism, we must also change the *Agent* subset of the model and build in a sufficient internal incentive to comply with moral rights. We will discuss this point further in Chapter 6 when we specify the moral conditions of economic efficiency. For now, all we need to see is that moral normative constraints can achieve what perfect information cannot. Therefore, moral normative constraints are missing conditions of the First Welfare Theorem.

Moral normative constraints as I have presented them involve both a moral rule and a sufficient internal incentive to comply with the moral rules. Both aspects are necessary. If we altered the agent set so that agents prefer moral visions of society or widely accepted moral virtues such as honesty and if we did not also introduce moral rules, agents may not achieve efficient outcomes of market interaction. As I will explain in detail in Chapter 6, agents must hold in common beliefs about which types of behaviors are required and which are prohibited to achieve the required social ordering of behavior. It is not sufficient if each agent is free to work toward whatever moral vision of society or whatever moral virtues she "prefers." Agents must also hold in common beliefs about how to hold each other responsible.

Summary

The argument of the previous section completes the line of argumentation begun earlier in the chapter. I have clarified the role of moral normative constraints in achieving Pareto-optimal equilibrium allocations. This has been accomplished by first placing a microeconomic model of social interaction within a broader framework of situational analysis to examine the institutional structure within which exchange takes place. In Chapter 2, we described a set of conventions that coordinate price-taking behavior (i.e., the Walrasian price mechanism). We have rigorously portrayed agents as being *strict rational egoists* in order to obtain a model of "pure selfishness." We have shown that, when a perfectly competitive market is understood, as it is in assumption (p_6), it is insufficient to ensure competitive behavior. Moral normative constraints are necessary conditions of competitive behavior. Therefore, since the First Fundamental Theorem of Welfare Economics establishes that efficient allocations of goods depend on every individual acting "competitively," moral normative constraints must be among its background assumptions.

Furthermore, moral normative constraints involve a sufficient internal incentive to comply with the rules. Strict rational egoists have no such incentives. Strict rational egoists will not comply with whatever rules are agreed upon, and the requisite means to internalize incidental and accidental externalities do not exist under Strict Rational Egoism.

Therefore, purely selfish people pursuing their own interests cannot achieve economic efficiency. It follows from this that the common understanding of the Invisible Hand Claim is incorrect.

4

A Spontaneous Order Objection

Can a population of strict rational egoists achieve efficient allocations of commodities through market interaction in the absence of moral normative constraints? The answer is, "No." We could now move on to our second central question:

What are the moral normative constraints and other types of normative conditions of market interaction leading to efficient outcomes?

However, I want to establish a stronger claim regarding the possibilities of purely selfish agents. I further claim that, given a class of situations fully described by assumptions (p_1)–(p_9), strict rational egoists cannot achieve Pareto-optimal equilibrium allocations of commodities at all.To refute this claim, one must show that, under Strict Rational Egoism, a regularity in social behavior could emerge spontaneously from the interactions of purely selfish agents – a regularity that enables efficient outcomes of trade. Thus, we have the following objection to my stronger claim:

If selfish individuals are construed to pursue their own interests from an initial setting in which moral normative constraints are absent and individuals' preferences only range over social states defined by allocations of consumption bundles, their behavior will coordinate into regular patterns (describable as being guided by rules), which in turn will be sufficient to produce optimal outcomes of trade.

I will refer to this objection as the Spontaneous Order Objection. [It is important to bear in mind that this is not a denial of the claim that some type of moral normative constraints are necessary conditions of Pareto efficiency. Rather, it denies that Pareto-optimal equilibrium allocations are not achievable for strict rational egoists in a social situation defined by assumptions (p_1)–(p_9).] If efficient outcomes of trade are not achievable for strict rational egoists, then the *situation* subset must be revised to include moral rules of some kind and the *agent* set must be revised to include a sufficient internal incentive to comply with the necessary rules. But then, of course, agents are not purely selfish and there are moral rules held in common. Pure selfishness cannot achieve a common good.

The claim expressed by the Spontaneous Order Objection is similar, but not identical, to the central position of the so-called spontaneous order tradition beginning with the eighteenth-century Scottish moral philosophers David Hume (1739) and Adam Ferguson (1767), continuing in the works of the nineteenth-century economist Carl Menger (1981[1871]), and extending at least through the writings of F. A. Hayek (1964) and Robert Sugden (1989).

However, a very important difference between the characterization of agents in the spontaneous order tradition and in our model must be kept in mind. In the spontaneous order tradition, agents are either human beings or rational egoists; in our model, agents are strict rational egoists. Therefore, although we will refer to this claim as the Spontaneous Order Objection to highlight its pertinence to our claim that strict rational egoists cannot achieve Pareto-optimal equilibrium allocations of commodities, and although we refer to these theorists' ideas to explicate certain concepts, we do not construe any particular theorist in that tradition as raising this particular question.

The Spontaneous Order Objection fails ultimately because it does not adequately differentiate between types of social situations. In his analysis of the spontaneous order tradition, Viktor Vanberg (1994: 65) wrote,

In view of the failure of the spontaneous order tradition to account adequately for the fundamental difference between co-ordination rules, like rules of language or rules of the road, and PD rules, like rules of morals, it cannot be emphasized strongly enough that an explanation of the first type of rules cannot be considered simply a model for an explanation of the second type.

However, even though Vanberg offers an account of the difference between the two types of rules, he does not offer an analysis of the two types of situations from which the rules are thought to emerge. In keeping with the analytical framework within which we are working, we trace the difference in the two types of rules to differences in situations. We then attempt to show that markets are institutions – that is, they are normative frameworks – that involve two kinds of norms: normative constraints and conventions. *Normative constraints* are solutions to what are called collective action situations, and *conventions* are solutions to coordination situations. We will argue that solutions to coordination situations are not constraints on maximizing behavior and, thus, could not function as normative constraints.[1]

The Conflation of Classes of Situations
by Hume, Menger, and Hayek

In his *A Treatise of Human Nature,* David Hume (1975: xvii) aspired to "explain the principles of human nature . . . built on a foundation (of) . . . experience and observation." Thus, in constructing an account of the emergence of the ideas of justice and of property, he describes a set of relevant aspects of a single type of situation out of which the ideas in question emerge. Hume (1975: 490) offered three examples (i.e., rowing a boat, using a language, or using a medium of exchange) which are actions within situations of a similar class. He wrote,

Two men, who pull the oars of a boat, do it by an agreement or convention, tho' they have never given promises to each other. Nor is the rule concerning the stability of the possession the less deriv'd from human conventions, that it arises gradually, and acquires force by a slow progression, and by our repeated experience of the inconveniences of transgressing it. On the contrary, this experience assures us still more, that the sense of interest has become common to all our fellows, and gives us a confidence of the future regularity of their conduct: And 'tis only on the expectation of this, that our moderation and abstinence are founded. In like manner are languages gradually establish'd by human conventions without any promise. In like manner do gold and silver become the common measures of exchange, and as esteem'd sufficient payment for what is a hundred times their value.

After this convention, concerning the abstinence from the possessions of others, is enter'd into, and every one has acquir'd a stability in his possessions, there immediately arise the ideas of justice and injustice; and also those of *property, right,* and *obligation.*

To anticipate the argument of the next section, imagine the people rowing the boat sitting next to each other. The preferences of both coordinate: They both desire a social state within which it is possible for both to be satisfied. Notice that the strategies they respectively adopt also coordinate: they each believe that they must row in synchrony with the other; neither of their strategies renders the other strategy ineffective. Finally, notice that the "inconveniences of transgressing" the joint strategy means the failure of both to satisfy their desires. The situations for which rowing a boat, using a language, or using a medium of exchange involve coordinative strategies adopted to achieve coordinative preferences are all of the same class. They are pure coordination situations.

However, the situations in which observing a set of property rights is the appropriate joint strategy is essentially different from these examples. In the next section, I clarify the difference. For the remainder of this section, I simply observe that several theorists have conflated two essentially different kinds of situations in their accounts of the "spontaneous" or "organic" emergence of rules.

In sum, we are not concerned with any particular aspect of the type of social situation that Hume described other than to call attention to the fact that he conflates two different types of situations. In the following sections, we analyze these types of situations and show how their conflation erroneously leads to the supposition that strict rational egoists could spontaneously generate a set of norms that make efficient trade possible. In particular we show that the "inconveniences of transgressing" a norm associated with one type of situation are distinct from the inconveniences of transgressing the other. Only one type of inconvenience provides a coordinative incentive. An individual, self-defeating inconvenience always results from taking a purely selfish action.

Hume seems to have set a precedent, thereby inaugurating a tradition in which other theorists continue to conflate these two types of situations. For example, Menger (1981: 262) wrote, "Money is not the product of an agreement on the part of economizing men nor the product of legislative acts. No one invented it." In this claim, he agreed with Hume: Using money is a joint strategy designed for a particular type of situation. Moreover, following Hume's example, Menger grouped together two types of situations that are essentially distinct. He claimed (1985: 147),

Law, language, the state, money, markets, all these social structures in their various empirical forms and in their constant change are to no small extent the *unintended* [emphasis added] result of social development. . . . Also understanding of them . . . must be analogous to the understanding of *unintentionally created social institutions* [emphasis added]. The solution of the most important problems of the theoretical sciences in general and of theoretical economics in particular is thus closely connected with the question of theoretically understanding the origin and change of *'organically' created social structures* [emphasis added].

Menger's grouping together the institutions of law, language, the state, money, and markets into a single broad class characterized as unintentionally created indicates that he also conflates the broad classes of situations from which they are claimed spontaneously to emerge.

F. A. Hayek (1964: 5) followed Menger's conflation of classes of situations in his discussion of the "useful institutions . . . such as language, morals, law, writing or money," which he treats as members of the same broad class of institution.

Categorizing Types of Social Situations

To reiterate, my claim is that economically efficient allocations of commodities are not achievable for strict rational egoists at all. The Spontaneous Order Objection to my claim is that a regularity in social behavior could emerge spontaneously from the interactions of strict rational egoists, which enable them to achieve economically efficient allocations of commodities. A crucial factor – perhaps *the* crucial factor – required to settle the question is the difference between interpretations of the set of conditions within which individuals act. Therefore, to refute the Spontaneous Order Objection, we first address the problem of categorizing social situations:

> *What is the best or proper or most conceptually useful way to differentiate between types of social situations for understanding what is required for efficient outcomes from trade that does not also unacceptably skew the resulting taxonomy?*

Four types of social situations are usually discussed in the relevant literature: (1) coordination situations, (2) collective action (Prisoners' Dilemma, PD) situations,[2] (3) inequality-preserving situations, and (4) cooperative-game situations.[3]

We are interested in situations in which assumptions (p_1)–(p_9) hold. Since the situation defined by premises (p_1)–(p_9) is noncooperative, (4) is not relevant. Since there are no rules, there exist no institutions that distribute advantages, and therefore, (3) is also not relevant. Therefore we are left with only two possible basic types of situations. We require a basis on which to differentiate between them that proves useful to further analysis.

Consider the following definitions representing one common type of taxonomy:

Coordination Situation. A *coordination situation* is any situation in which successful rational utility-maximizing behavior under strategic, noncooperative conditions yields a strictly Pareto-superior result.

Collective Action Situation. A *collective action situation* is any situation in which rational utility-maximizing behavior under strategic, noncooperative conditions yields a Pareto-inferior result.[4]

Notice that types of situations are determined by types of outcomes under this taxonomy. Because these definitions are outcome based, they fail to state precisely the conditions that lead to the outcomes. Since understanding and solving problems requires one to pay attention to their precipitating conditions, overlooking this distinction can lead to an erroneous analysis.

Russell Hardin (1988) offered a five-part taxonomy: (pure) conflict, (pure) coordination, and mixed motive. It implicitly includes a basis for differentiating classes of social situations. But, in explicating what he sees as the "strategic structures of categories of interactions," Russell Hardin (1988: 31) categorized types of noncooperative games. Even though Hardin (1988: 32) categorized types of noncooperative games, he also claimed that game theory is "badly named: it has little or nothing to do with games, and it is hardly a theory. It is preeminently a descriptive framework for categorizing social interactions."

However, situations cannot be adequately described by game matrices. Ostrom et al. (1994: 27) observed that "the issue of rule-breaking and rule enforcing cannot be addressed by a noncooperative game model." Furthermore, Field (1984: 687) wrote:

even "non-cooperative games" contain, as part of their description, certain rules adherence to which is assumed as part of the analysis. Although *additional* cooperation is precluded by the assumption that the game is "non-cooperative," the very fact that interaction can be described and perceived as a game is evidence of rudimentary structure of interaction.

Even though situations do entail a certain range of physical constraints that can be modeled game-theoretically, this will not escape Field's criticism. Ostrom et al. (1994: 26) observed that "game theory does not distinguish between the types of constraints that affect the structure of a game."[5]

Therefore, we need a basis for a taxonomy of classes of social situations that allows for rule breaking and, therefore, for strategy sets that are not predelimited (i.e., natural strategy domains) and that cannot inadvertently fail to maintain a distinction between positive and normative constraints.

An Alternative Basis for Differentiating Classes of Social Situations

No types of conditions that determine opportunities and possible outcomes are as pertinent to a taxonomy of initial situations as are agents' preferences and the means (actions or strategies) they take to satisfy them, which in turn are determined in part by the constraints agents face and the domain of their preferences (i.e., the set of alternative social states over which their preferences range). Notice that no premise in the assumption set, that is, nothing in Strict Rational Egoism requires the compatibility of different agents' preferences or of their strategies to achieve those preferences. Given the assumption of normative individualism, it is a matter of accident whether or not preferences and strategies are compatible. For the sake of more precision, I use the terms *coordinate* and *conflict*. We first attempt to make these distinctions explicit.

If preference relations are independent and an individual attempts to actualize a desired social state, she is indifferent to features other than those that make that social state desirable to her. Therefore, if two individuals desire the same social state, it is possible that both can be satisfied because it is possible that the features that make that social state desirable for either individual are irrelevant to the other. In fact, an outcome of trade is some social state in which the commodities obtained by some individual were sold by the other.

Therefore, to say that preferences coordinate is to say that, for any two agents, there is at least one social state that they both prefer the most. To say that preferences coordinate is not to say that agents adopt the same preference relation but that they are compatible at the most preferred social state. The idea of coordinative preferences is instantiated by, for example, two agents simultaneously approaching an intersection and each desiring to get through the intersection without colliding with another car: each agent prefers that state of affairs in which each has crossed the intersection without harm. It is mistaken to conceive of it as that one achieved in the least time. Time of achievement is a matter of strategy.

To say that preferences conflict is to say that, if some desired state of affairs obtains for some agent, some desire cannot be fulfilled for some other agent. For example, if two people each attend a Bonsai sale and prefer a social state defined in part by each valuing a particular Bonsai at the same price and in part by the presence of that particular Bonsai in her yard, then, if either agent achieves her desires, the other cannot. For another example, suppose that two individuals prefer to consume the same banana, say, only because they wanted a banana and there was only one left in the produce section. For one agent to prefer a social state in which she consumes a particular banana is perforce to prefer a social state in which every other agent is excluded from consuming that same banana.

Similarly, strategies that agents choose to satisfy their preferences may coordinate or conflict. Two strategies coordinate just in case, if both were taken, both agents would achieve their desired social state. Two strategies conflict just in case the success of either strategy renders the other ineffective. Strategies may conflict intentionally or nonintentionally. Recall that a strategy is a course of action. An *intentional conflict* of strategies occurs when at least one individual deliberately hinders the actions of some other agent. *Nonintentional conflicts* of strategies occur when some agent's action foils the efforts of some other agent accidentally, mistakenly, inadvertently, carelessly, involuntarily, or unintentionally.[6] We, therefore, refine our definitions based on these considerations:

Coordination Situation. An initial situation is a *coordination situation* if and only if, given agents' constraints and the domain of preferences,

    (1) their preferences coordinate, and
    (2) at least one of their strategies coordinate.

Notice that, in a coordination situation, every agent most highly prefers the same social state. But only when they choose coordinative strategies does successful rational utility-maximizing behavior yield a Pareto-optimal outcome. Thus, even though this account agrees with Hardin's in that successful rational utility-maximizing behavior under strategic, noncooperative conditions[7] yields a strictly Pareto-superior result, it gives the necessary and sufficient conditions of such a result.

Collective Action Situation. An initial situation is a *collective action situation* if and only if, given agents' constraints and the domain of preferences, even though at least one of their preferences coordinate, their strategies conflict.

Again, our alternative definition of a collective action situation is compatible with Hardin's account, in that successful rational utility-maximizing behavior yields Pareto-inferior outcomes. However, rational utility-maximizing behavior is possibly successful only when strategies do not conflict. But then, this means that both preferences and strategies must coordinate. In other words, the initial situation, in effect, must be converted from a collective action situation into a coordination situation by rendering a previously most highly preferred social state unattainable.

There are only four possible types of situations, given agents' constraints and the domain of preferences:

(1) At least one of each agent's preferences coordinates and each agent's best strategy coordinates with every other agent's best strategy.
(2) At least one of each agent's preferences coordinates, but each agent's best strategy conflicts with every other agent's best strategies.
(3) All of each agent's preferences conflict, but each agent's best strategy coordinates with every other agent's best strategy.
(4) Each agent's preferences and best strategies conflict.

I defined *coordination situation* to cover case (1) and *collective action situation* to cover case (2). Cases (3) and (4) are moot since no preferences coordinate.

One reason to categorize social situations is to discover solutions to those situations that present problems to a group of agents, each pursuing their desires and preferring the best outcome. As long as it is possible that strategies conflict, it is possible that some agent will fail to achieve her goals, and it is possible that some convention or normative constraint could provide success for each agent by restricting agents' natural strategy domains.[8]

Solutions to situations of the second type are normative constraints. Normative constraints convert collective action situations into coordination situations. Recall that a *normative constraint,* in general, is a rule that effectively prevents some type of action from occurring by virtue of a corresponding enforcement mechanism that supplies sufficient incentives in some way or other, which render the action undesirable, thereby effectively inhibiting its occurrence.

Hence, we see that there are only two basic types of strategic noncooperative social situations in which a possible regularity in social behavior can achieve the best outcome – coordination situations and collective action situations. The two types are differentiated on the basis of the preferences and strategies of agents. The rules that regulate behavior so that the results are Pareto optimal differ according to the type of incentive to comply. Incentives to comply with solutions to unconverted coordination situations are purely rational. Incentives to comply with solutions to coordination situations that have been converted from collective action situations are both normative and rational.

Conventions Are Not Normative Constraints

Notice that a solution to a coordination is not a particular strategy. It is a rule (or set of rules) with respect to possible strategies. For example, when two agents each prefer to cross an intersection without collision, they must still decide how to achieve it. Their respective preferences coordinate. Thus, each agent must choose one strategy from a set of possible options. In this example, consider just two: each agent could decide either to cross immediately upon arrival or to let whoever arrived first cross first. Given the derived principle for action, agents will agree to the first option because they will have good reason to believe that such a means is the best way to achieve their goals. Their joint strategy can be expressed by the rule: Whoever gets to the intersection first, crosses first.[9] Neither agent is constrained by the rule, given that their preferences coordinate and that they choose coordinative strategies by (DPA). Agents would reject an alternative strategy because they have good reason to expect an accident or personal harm of some kind. But if they take turns based on whoever arrives at the intersection first, they have good reason to believe that they will cross safely, which is their most highly preferred social state. Therefore, solutions to coordination problems are not constraints on maximizing behavior; the best feasible means is the one they take. Solutions to situations of type (1) are conventions, not normative constraints, because agents have an incentive to comply with the relevant rule based solely on their instrumental rationality. Every other alterative strategy in automatically unfeasible.

The Requisite Normative Constraints Cannot Emerge within a Population of Strict Rational Egoists

By definition, instrumental, utility-maximizing behavior in collective action situations by strict rational egoists inevitably results in Pareto-inferior social states and can lead to strictly Pareto-inferior social states unless their actions are normatively constrained. The Spontaneous Order Objection depends on agents being able to institute such constraints from collective action situations described by assumptions (p_1)–(p_9). Thus,

> If exchange situations are collective action situations and solutions to collective action situations cannot spontaneously emerge among strict rational egoists, the Spontaneous Order Objection fails.

All we have shown thus far is that some spontaneous order theorists have failed to make a crucial distinction between types of situations and that it is, therefore, a mistake to generalize from coordination situations to collective action situations. We have yet to show both that exchange situations are collective action situations and that there is no spontaneous solution to collective action situations for strict rational egoists. In the next sections, we first offer an explicit description of an exchange situation and show that it is a collective action situation. I then examine possible solutions to collective action situations and show that none can emerge among a population of strict rational egoists.

An Exchange Situation Is a Collective Action Situation

Are exchange situations coordination situations or collective action situations? An *exchange situation* is defined by the set of assumptions (p_1)–(p_9). This means that although conventions that equilibrate supply and demand are involved, no moral rules constrain agents' natural strategy domains. It would be confusing at best to think that markets, which are conceived as institutional frameworks for trade and which include both conventions and normative constraints, are involved in exchange situations. Thus, an exchange situation is a situation in which agents are rational utility-maximizers having independent preference relations; agents act under strategic, noncooperative conditions free from normative constraints; each agent controls a finite endowment of commodities with preferences ranging over alternative consumption bundles; information is logically maximal; and proposing or accepting an exchange is only one of several available strategies. An exchange situation is one in which at least one of each agent's preferences coordinates, but each agent's best strategy conflicts with every other agent's best strategies because there are no normative constraints precluding force or fraud. Since a conflict of strategies defines a collective action situation, an exchange situation is therefore a collective action situation.

Solutions to Collective Action Situations Cannot Spontaneously Emerge among Strict Rational Egoists

We begin by considering five possible types of solutions to collective action situations.[10]

1. *Dual utility solution.* Agents are both egoistic and altruistic. Each person has both private preferences and social preferences. Therefore, each individual can be characterized by two related preference relations. An individual forgoes a utility-maximizing strategy if and only if her social preference overrides her private preferences.[11]
2. *Moral principle solution.* An agent unilaterally and rationally elects to act on some set of moral principles. For example, an agent either takes an action or refrains from it either because she generalizes her prospective action

or because she calculates the alternatives looking for which action generates the greatest happiness for the greatest number.

3. *Iteration-dependent solution.* Agents have good reason to believe that the situation they face will be repeated indefinitely. They will, therefore, either discount the future or adopt a tit-for-tat strategy.[12]

4. *Hobbesian solution.* Agents intentionally institute a set of rules enforced by the State, legal normative constraints.

5. *Morality solution.* Regardless of how it may emerge, morality, construed as a social practice involving a self-enforced set of procedural rights or rules in addition to a minimal set of substantive rights or rules, normatively constrains individuals' actions.[13]

Since we portray exchange situations as devoid of moral normative constraints, a solution to an exchange situation must not assume either of the two aspects of a moral normative constraint.[14] The dual utility solution can succeed only by altering assumptions within the *Agent's* subset. Similarly, the moral principle solution is not available because it involves the selection of a decision rule which we have excluded by assumption (p_6.) That leaves us with the iteration-dependent solution, the Hobbesian solution, and the morality solution.

Several theorists believe that the iterated Prisoners' Dilemma models real-life collective action problems and try to determine whether an internal solution could emerge when the situation is iterated.[15] To examine closely the iteration-dependent solution, we describe the Prisoners' Dilemma. Two resistance fighters are caught. Their captors separate them and present each with the following:

> We are giving each of you a choice between confessing and not confessing. If you both keep silent, each of you will each spend 1 year in prison. If both of you confess, you will each get 3 years. But if, on the other hand, one of you confesses and the other keeps silent, we will let the confessor go and give the silent one 5 years.

Each prisoner reasons that his best strategy is to confess, which results in each spending 3 years in prison. Individual, utility-maximizing behavior leads to Pareto-inferior outcomes, indeed a strictly Pareto-inferior outcome. Everyone would prefer at least one other outcome to the actual. Alternatively, even though at least one of each agent's preferences coordinate, each agent's best strategy conflicts with every other agent's best strategies.

Now, under what conditions is a collective action situation repeated? Before we can determine the conditions of iteration, we must clarify what is meant by situation iteration. There are two views on what it means to iterate a collective action situation. On the first view, in the real world a situation is not strictly duplicated, but rather a similar situation emerges later. John goes to Acme Used Cars and talks with salesperson Theresa. Two years later, Jim (who is John's friend) goes to Acme Used Cars and talks to salesperson Theresa. Some features of the first situation are absent from the second situation. On the second view, the same situation is exactly duplicated after its first outcome is nullified. The situation is iterated only if a regulative rule is introduced into the Normative Conditions subset, which indicates that no outcome is final.[16]

An argument based on the first view fails. First, it is mistaken to cite how PD situations frequently recur in the real world. More importantly, we are rigorously eliminating the effect of moral normative constraints on individuals so that agents in our model are not human beings. Until we can determine what strict rational egoists can achieve, empirical models are premature. Second, we have already shown that strict rational egoists will always choose the best feasible means to achieve their most highly valued social state, so when similar situations emerge inefficient outcomes result. An argument based on the second view will fail also because, under Strict Rational Egoism, there is no such a regulative rule.

In sum, the dual utility solution requires that we abandon assumption (p_1). The moral principle solution also requires that we abandon assumption (p_6). The iteration-dependent solution, the Hobbesian solution, and the morality solution each require that we abandon assumption (p_8). Therefore, there are no solutions to collective action situations for strict rational egoists because each requires a change in at least one of assumptions (p_1)–(p_9).

We have not yet refuted the Spontaneous Order Objection. A spontaneous order solution might not initially require an alteration in the description of agents, nor must it presuppose a set of rules. The Objection only claims that, on the grounds of assumptions (p_1)–(p_9), normative constraints can emerge. Thus, the unworkability of imposing an existing solution does not entail the impossibility of spontaneous order. In other words, for the Spontaneous Order Objection to hold, a regularity in social behavior guided by rules must emerge from a situation described by assumptions (p_1)–(p_9).

A social order requisite for efficient outcomes of trade could emerge only if agents can agree on and comply with rules. There are only two kinds of rules: conventions that apply to coordination situations and rules that apply to collective action situations. If agents agree on a convention, the convention cannot convert a collective action situation into a coordination situation because it does not apply. It cannot apply to a collective action situation because, by definition, collective action situations involve alternative feasible strategies and agents are compelled by the derived principle for action to take the best of the alternatives over what the convention indicates. If agents agree on a rule that applies to collective actions situations, they have an incentive not to comply with such rules and have no incentive to comply with such rules. Furthermore, strict rational egoists cannot alter their motivations; moral motivations cannot develop from pure selfishness. Let us consider this in more detail.

Ullmann-Margalit (1977: 22,28) wrote, "only a norm backed by sanctions" or a "norm . . . supported by sufficiently severe sanctions" is capable of solving collective action problems. She describes a simple two-step procedure by which rational individuals are supposed to find a solution. They first portray the joint strategy which achieves the Pareto-superior outcome as being obligatory and then they institute by agreement a rule to that effect. Suppose arguendo that a regulative rule is agreed upon to iterate Prisoners' Dilemma situations and that a set of rules that constitutes a Hobbesian solution are instituted. In both cases agents must agree on an enforcement mechanism designed to prevent defection. In his discussion of solutions to collective action situations, Taylor indicated that external solutions can be either centralized or decentralized. These types are two poles of a continuum from perfectly centralized to perfectly decentralized. Taylor (1990: 225) wrote,

A solution is *decentralized* to the extent that the initiative for the changes in possibilities, attitudes, or beliefs that constitute an external solution is dispersed amongst the members of the group; or, the greater the proportion of the group's members involved in solving the collective action problem (for example, applying sanctions to free-riders), the more decentralized the solution. Contrariwise, a solution is *centralized* to the extent that such involvement is concentrated in the hands of only a few members of the group.

If a centralized enforcement mechanism is agreed to, individuals charged with enforcement face a second-order collective action situation. They have an incentive not to fulfill their obligations. For example, in some marijuana-growing countries, police charged with enforcing laws against growing marijuana have an incentive not to fulfill their obligation because an alternative feasible strategy is to grow it themselves. If they were strict rational egoists, they would in fact not fulfill their obligations. On the other hand, if enforcement is decentralized and placed into the hands of all individuals, everyone faces a second-order collective action situation because everyone will have an incentive to "free-ride." That is, agents have an incentive not to expend the effort to enforce a rule, thinking someone else will. In either case, for there spontaneously to emerge an enforcement mechanism sufficient for the iteration-dependent solution and the Hobbesian solution, agents would have to act contrary to (DPA). Only if agents themselves are motivated for reasons other than pure selfishness will they comply with constraints on their actions. However, strict rational egoists are motivated only by purely selfish reasons. The spontaneous order of markets is supposed by the Spontaneous Order Objection to emerge from a situation described by assumptions (p_1)–(p_9). But, since strict rational egoists will not comply with a set of rules, even if such rules could be agreed on, there can be no solution, and, thus, the Spontaneous Order Objection fails.

Alternative Accounts of Spontaneous Order

There are several accounts of spontaneous order, which may be thought to conflict with the result we have obtained. However, careful examination of such accounts shows that often they do not apply at all. They do not apply either because they are based on empirical evidence, in which case there is no reason to think that agents are purely selfish, or because they are based on theoretical accounts in which agents are not purely selfish. It is important always to bear in mind that we have rigorously excluded moral factors to determine what can be achieved by agents who are purely selfish. Consider the following three examples. The first two do not apply and the third is insufficient.

Robert Sugden (1989) argued that rudimentary property rights can emerge without explicit agreement as a solution to a coordination problem by citing empirical evidence. However, in basing his claim on empirical evidence, it cannot be determined whether individuals in the case study were strict rational egoists. We do not know whether some internalized norm or pattern affected agents' behavior in the cases he cites. We risk introducing norms into the model if we do not make our case only on the grounds of the model. Thus, the objection does not apply to our model.

Robert Nozick (1974) offered a theoretical account of the spontaneous emergence of a minimal state. His model is discordant with my model in three ways. First, he begins (1974: 5) with a "most favored situation of anarchy" in which "people generally satisfy moral constraints and generally act as they ought." He attempts to describe how a state would arise spontaneously from such a state of nature. Second, individuals in Nozick's initial situation have well-defined rights and are aware of them. Last, they may also possess a wide range of moral motivations. Therefore, Nozick's agents have not been rigorously evacuated of all moral constraint. Spontaneous emergence of a solution to collective action situations in Nozick's account are not subject to the constraints we have imposed. Thus, an objection based on Nozick's account does not apply to our model.

Jean Hampton (1997) showed how *rational egoists* can create a minimal state and thereby escape a Hobbesian state of nature. The social order thus established does not involve moral rules, and Hampton's agents' motives to comply are not moral. We saw in Chapter 3 that both elements (which comprise moral normative constraints) are required. Furthermore, her "morally-justified political authority" cannot bear the weight of enforcing moral rules even if they were to agree on them. Even if Hampton's agents institute a group of enforcers of some kind whose role is to detect and enforce compliance with moral rules designed to permit the achievement of economic efficiency, and even if there is some way to "enforce" the enforcers, that is, to make sure they do not shirk or free-ride, it will not be sufficient. Many nonmarket actions cannot be detected. For example, no one could detect the "false offer curve" discussed in Chapter 3. In other words, unless everyone has sufficient internal incentives to comply with moral rules, the "weight" of compliance in such an enforced social order falls on what amounts to a legal system that depends on its ability to detect. The pervasive indetectability of some actions cannot be mitigated under Hampton's account. We must realize that it is not Hampton's intention to show that social order sufficient to ensure that efficient outcomes of trade can emerge spontaneously from a population of strict rational egoists. Thus, an objection based on Jean Hamptons' theoretical account of spontaneous order cannot succeed against the result we have obtained for Strict Rational Egoism.

Summary Discussion

In Chapter 3, we showed that moral normative constraints are necessary conditions of Pareto-optimal allocations. Our principal guiding question in this chapter has been:

What if it could be shown that, under assumptions (p_1)–(p_9), a regularity in social behavior could emerge spontaneously from the interactions of selfish agents, which enables efficient outcomes of trade?

I have presented a three-step argument showing that there are no spontaneous solutions to exchange situations for strict rational egoists. First, I demonstrated that exchange situations are collective action situations. I then showed that there are no solutions to collective action situations for strict rational egoists that do not require an alteration of Strict Rational Egoism. Pareto-optimal outcomes can, therefore, only be achieved in collective action situations when moral normative constraints are in place. Finally, I demonstrated that, since strict rational egoists will not comply with the necessary constraints nor with an obligation to enforce them, strict rational egoists cannot institute the requisite system of moral normative constraints. Therefore, strict rational egoists cannot achieve Pareto-optimal allocations through trade.

5

The Roles of Moral Normative Constraints in Relation to Externalities

Recall that there are three reasons why a population of strict rational egoists cannot achieve efficient allocations in the absence of moral normative constraints. In Chapter 3, we saw that moral normative constraints are necessary conditions. This reason is sufficient in itself to establish the claim. In Chapter 4, we saw that strict rational egoists cannot institute the required moral rules. In this chapter, I establish that the requisite means to internalize incidental and accidental externalities do not exist under Strict Rational Egoism.

The proof of the First Welfare Theorem in Chapter 2 presupposes that externalities are absent. However, assuming that externalities are absent sets the question of the role of moral normative constraints aside, just as does assuming that every agent behaves competitively. Therefore, we cannot simply assume that externalities are absent. We must determine what normative conditions are required either to preclude or to rectify externalities so as to achieve economic efficiency. To proceed, I first clarify the term *externality* and distinguish between *intentional, accidental,* and *incidental externalities.* I then discuss four roles of moral normative constraints and conventions for eliminating externalities.

Externality

Many theorists have noted that the notions *market failure* and *externality* are not well defined. Kenneth Arrow (1969: 133) wrote that "nowhere in the literature does there appear to be a clear general definition of [market failure] or the more general one of 'externality'." Andreas A. Papandreou (1994: 2) wrote,

Given the importance of externality in economic theory, and the effort put into characterizing externality, it is surprising how hazy a concept it has remained. Extending the empty box metaphor, not only has there not been consensus on what externality should signify, but the box seems to be semi-opaque, preventing a clear understanding of what the different ideas are. The present intuitive notion of externality as activities that take place outside market transactions, belies the difficulties that arise the minute one tries to give analytical content to this intuition, treating it as a separate category of market failure.

A good definition is found in Mas-Colell et al. (1995: 352): "an *externality* is present whenever the well-being of a consumer or the production possibilities of a firm are directly affected by the actions of another agent in the economy." But even this definition omits certain essential components.

To understand the roles of moral normative constraints for eliminating externalities, we must recognize three types of externalities: *intentional, accidental,* and *incidental.*[1] Acts of theft and fraud directly affect the well-being of consumers and exemplify *intentional externalities.* Harm resulting from negligence or from an accident exemplifies an *accidental externality.* Externalities also include *incidental* effects of the acts of production and consumption. Thus, we settle on the following definition:

Externality. An *externality* is an uncompensated cost or benefit that may be intentional, accidental, or incidental.

Most accounts of the First Welfare Theorem assume that externalities are absent. By presupposing the absence of externalities, their absence is a necessary condition for Pareto-optimal equilibrium allocations just as moral normative constraints are necessary conditions. Notice the striking similarity in the work being done by the two assumptions. Moral normative constraints preclude the inefficient *consequences of intentional nonmarket actions* by precluding the action itself. To assume the absence of externalities simply rules out the inefficient consequences of *any* nonmarket action. Both assumptions are designed to rule out inefficient allocations of commodities by ruling out social states that are inefficient, where such social states are the consequences of actions.[2] Thus, in both cases, strict rational egoists can achieve efficient outcomes in market interaction only if some kinds of effects of their actions are precluded or rectified.

This similarity in the effects of the two assumptions raises several questions. What is the relationship between the *presence of moral normative constraints* and the *absence of externalities?* We have seen that the idea is to rule out the uncompensated consequences of actions. Can an adequate set of moral normative constraints at least do some of the work that the *absence of externalities* is intended to do? On the other hand, what assurance do we have that solutions to externalities do not conflict with some particular moral normative constraint? Conversely, what is the relationship between the *presence* of externalities and the *absence* of moral normative constraints? Clearly, in both cases individuals' actions can directly affect the utility of others without being mediated by the market (i.e., without others being compensated).

To assume that all externalities are absent and that every agent behaves competitively is to set aside the question of the role of morality. The system of moral normative constraints presented in Chapter 6 secures competitive behavior and eliminates intentional externalities but makes no provision for the internalization of accidental and incidental externalities. Nevertheless, a system of other normative conditions can rectify the effects of nonintentional externalities and provide procedures for internalizing incidental externalities so that individuals can achieve Pareto-optimal equilibrium allocations.

The Roles of Moral Normative Constraints in Achieving Economic Efficiency

(1) A system of moral normative constraints precludes externalities due to intentional consequences of nonmarket action.

(2) A system of moral normative constraints and conventions rectifies accidental and incidental externalities.

(3) Moral normative constraints and conventions coordinate expectations and thereby reduce transaction costs.

(4) Moral normative constraints are the logical limits of the commodification of desire.

We have established the first claim. Claims (2) and (3) are based on the general goals of tort law, property law, and contract law, respectively, and have been established. However, it remains a matter of further research to specify the moral content of such constraints. In the following discussions, I argue for claim (4) and in so doing show the relevance of the inalienability of a right to autonomy. In a landmark paper on market failure and externalities, Kenneth Arrow (1969: 147, 8) wrote,

There is one deep problem in the interpretation of externalities that can only be signaled here. What aspects of others' behavior do we consider as affecting a utility function? . . . Do we extend the concept of externality to all matters that an individual cares about? Or, in the spirit of John Stuart Mill, is there a second-order value judgment which excludes some of these preferences from the formation of social policy as being legitimate infringements of individual liberty?

Let us probe this "deep problem in the interpretation of externalities," which Arrow only "signaled." Of course, this will involve reference to the concept of an externality. Arrow raised three related questions, which clearly suggest that a precise concept of an externality must include a clear account of the role of moral normative constraints:

(1) What aspects of others' behavior do we consider as affecting a utility function?

(2) Do we extend the concept of externality to all matters that an individual cares about?

(3) Is there a second-order value judgment that excludes some of these preferences from the formation of social policy as being legitimate infringements of individual liberty?

Consider question (1). Arrow's revealed-preference approach to the question suggests that we can identify those aspects of behavior that affect the utility functions of others if we have a way of determining the conditions under which an individual's utility function is affected. Obviously, an individual's market interaction reveals his preference. However, we are concerned with phenomena that escape the price mechanism. Arrow cited the general case in which one individual's supporting legislation that controls another individual's behavior indicates that the second individual's behavior itself, in addition to perhaps the effects of such behavior, affects the utility function of the first person. He then cited two instances of the general case. Legislation intended to control "homosexuality" and "drug-taking" indicates that the utility function of the individuals supporting the legislation is affected. But just how is it affected? As Arrow added, these behaviors do not directly affect anyone else not engaged in them. There is no immediate physical or causal connection between the parties other than that one disapproves.[3] What, then, is the externality in these cases? Individuals who support the legislation prefer any set of social states in which the "commodities" obtained by the practice of homosexuality and drug-taking are absent to those defined in part by such commodities. Thus, we may conclude that others' behavior itself can affect someone's utility function as much as the consequences of others' behavior.

We commonly consider the consequences of others' actions as affecting others' utility functions. A consumption externality like smoking, for example, implies that the *effect* of some person's action (i.e., the creation of a smoke-polluted environment or the diseases that can result from exposure to second-hand smoke) alters another person's utility level and is itself unpriced. Therefore, some person's preferences range over states of affairs that are not definable in terms of ordinary consumption bundles.

To reiterate, there are at least two aspects of an individual's behavior that affect others' utility functions: the consequences of others' behavior and the behavior itself.

To internalize such aspects of behavior is to commodify these aspects. That is, were the behaviors themselves fully priced and traded, so that every party was compensated, the externality would be internalized. But when externalities are present such as those cited by Arrow, the domain of preferences is greater than the set of commodities. To internalize externalities is to increase the size of the set of commodities, that is, to "expand the commodity space." When consequences of individuals' actions that affect others (as in the smoking example) are commodified or when behaviors themselves that affect others' utility functions (as in the homosexuality example) are commodified, those utility-affecting consequences and that utility-affecting behavior are internalized. (Notice that this seems to make any undesirable action (or aspect of an action) a possible commodity that then can be priced and traded. It follows that even immoral behavior broadly seen as such can be acceptable when the "price is right" for everyone else. It is similar to the Medieval selling of indulgences.)

The concept of a commodity possibly requires redefinition whenever the commodity space is expanded and the domain of preferences is greater than the domain of commodities. Thus, when Arrow (1969: 46) wrote that "externalities can be regarded as ordinary commodities," the concept of a commodity is extended to include any factor that enters any agent's utility function, either favorably or unfavorably.[4] The commodification of some aspect of a social state that affects someone's utility function is the commodification of desire. A desire becomes commodified through a process of a social construction whereby it can be priced and traded. Thus, expanding the commodity set is tantamount to the commodification of desire.

This brings us to question (2): Do we extend the concept of externality to all matters that an individual cares about? Arrow implicitly concedes that the answer to (2) is negative, and that (3) stands for the conjecture that a value judgment is the only or proper limit on individuals' preferences. In the set of assumptions with which we have been working, there is no provision for the evaluation of preferences. Unless preferences themselves are subject to moral evaluation, limits on the domain of preferences can only be indirectly effected through limits on their commodification. We thus are led to probe more deeply the question concerning the role of moral normative constraints in relation to externalities: What limits the domain of preferences? Are there moral limits as Arrow conjectured?

Economists assume that every market failure can be explained as a failure to realize some assumption of the First Welfare Theorem. As Mas-Colell et al. (1995: 308) wrote,

In an important sense, the first fundamental welfare theorem establishes the perfectly competitive case as a benchmark for thinking about outcomes in market economies. In particular, any inefficiencies that arise in a market economy, and hence any role for Pareto-improving market intervention, *must* be traceable to a violation of at least one of the assumptions of this theorem.

Every policy prescription can be seen as an attempt to realize some assumption of the First Welfare Theorem. Given the "incomplete or absence of markets" concept of an externality, it follows that procedures used to correct market failure are, in effect, procedures for expanding the commodity space. Judge Richard Posner's property rights assignment principle is an example of a procedure that "internalizes" externalities by expanding the commodity space.

Posner's assignment principle must be understood within the context of his economics-based jurisprudence.[5] His economic approach to law[6] has both analytic and normative aspects. The economic analysis of law adopts a set of assumptions similar to Strict Rational Egoism.[7] On these assumptions, it provides a theory of legal behavior, legal systems, and legislation.

Posner's jurisprudence also has a normative aspect. Posner argues that courts *should* mimic market outcomes where feasible. For example, to find legal remedies in common law cases, courts should first attempt to mimic market outcomes understood as Kaldor-Hicks[8] efficient allocations of resources. Posner's argument can be abstracted from a longer, more involved discussion of common law. He observes that one part of common law, the law of property, is concerned with property rights defined as rights to the exclusive use of resources. Legal protection of property rights creates incentives to maximize value and to use resources efficiently. However, while a right to the exclusive use of property protected by law is a necessary condition for wealth maximization, it is not sufficient. Irrational economic behavior by owners of property may preclude its efficient use. Hence, efficiency requires that an irrational producer can be induced to transfer his property right to someone else.[9] Posner's normative jurisprudence depends on a seminal idea in the economic analysis of law called the *Coase Theorem*. Ronald Coase (1960) showed that when transactions are costless, information is sufficient, individuals act cooperatively, and income effects are absent, then markets will produce efficient allocations of resources. That is, no costs will be imposed on anyone not voluntarily receiving a benefit. Moreover, the market can achieve efficient solutions to externalities without state intervention and will achieve this result regardless of any initial assignment of legal entitlements. However, Coase showed that even under these conditions transaction costs may preclude the optimal use of resources primarily because they prevent voluntary exchange. Posner (1992: 52) claims that an important, but often overlooked feature of Coase's paper is that

The common law of nuisance can be understood as an attempt to increase the value of resource use by assigning the property right to the party to a conflicting land use to whom the right would be most valuable.

In other words, given the assumption that common law can be explained as the attempt to maximize wealth and that exclusive and transferable property rights are sufficient for the efficient use of resources were it not for transaction costs, courts should simply mimic market outcomes by assigning entitlements to those who would have valued them most where voluntary exchange is feasible.

Posner realizes that the assignment principle is not foolproof because it "ignores the costs of administering the property rights system" (1992: 52) and is difficult to apply in practice. Nevertheless, he accepts it as a normative principle because "in most cases, and without excessive cost, [courts] may be able to approximate the optimum definition of property rights, and these approximations may guide resource use more efficiently that would an economically random assignment of property rights" (1992: 53).

Posner's approach to internalizing externalities – that is, to commodifying desire – has important implications. In the abstract, there are no limits on what desires an agent can have, so there are no limits on the commodification of those desires. Arrow wondered if there are moral limits. In a famous paper on property law, Calabresi and Melamed (1972) suggested that inalienability rules, which are grounded in moral considerations, may limit the procedures for internalizing externalities. But Posner suggested that there are no limits except administrative costs.

Efficient allocations of commodities are possible only if individuals can take purposive action. Purposive action is possible only if each individual is treated as an agent. The idea of being "treated as an agent" must be understood in a context of a normative social practice. Recall from Chapter 1 that a *normative social practice* is a social phenomenon (a regularity in social behavior) (1) guided by beliefs held in common concerning (a) the criteria by which a group of individuals evaluate their own and others' behavior and according to which criteria they hold each other responsible and concerning (b) the procedures for holding each other responsible. An individual is treated as an agent when she is permitted to choose ends and courses of actions to achieve those ends, and when responses to agents are responses to her choices in light of commonly held criteria regarding behavior. A normative social practice presupposes that each agent knows what types of actions are proscribed or prescribed, the consequences of violation, and that each individual implicitly agrees both to guide her actions accordingly and to hold others accountable. Let us then understand a *right to autonomy* to be a right to be treated as an agent, that is, to be autonomous – to guide one's own actions within a circumscribed set of morally possible actions. A right to autonomy enables a normative social practice to exist. Since, as I shall argue in Chapter 6, a right to autonomy is inalienable, there are logical limits to procedures for internalizing externalities. The "incomplete markets" view of externalities implies that any aspect of any state of affairs, which is also the object of some agent's desire, is a tradable commodity. A logical limit would exist if some desire cannot be converted into commodities without undercutting the very conditions necessary for Pareto optimality. In other words, since externalities are internalized just in case the commodity space can be extended just in case the relevant desire can be commodified, if some desires cannot be converted into commodities without undercutting the very conditions that are necessary for complete efficiency, then we have discovered some logical limit to the commodification of desire which might apply to legal decisions.

In Chapter 6, I argue that a right to autonomy and Hohfeldian liberty with respect to defined commodities define an individual's liberty. Where a commodity is not defined, liberty with respect to that potential commodity is fully defined by a right to autonomy. Recall that there are no direct limitations on the domain of preferences. Therefore, behaviors and consequences of behaviors can become commodities. Now, consider two alternative social states, σ_n and σ_m. Social state σ_n is characterized in part by the fact that the total quantity of commodity m belongs to individual j. Social state σ_m is characterized in part by the fact that the total quantity of commodity m belongs to individual i. Suppose that σ_n is the current social state. Social state σ_m will be realized if and only if individual i values the total quantity of commodity m more than does individual j, and both can agree on an allocation of the cooperative surplus, which is the difference in the values each places on the commodity. There is nothing in this procedure to prevent the total quantity of commodity m from representing individual j's autonomy. For example, it is possible for an individual to sell herself into slavery or be forced into slavery, thereby effectively disregarding her own right to autonomy. Even though a slave's preferences continue to range over alternative social states, she is unable to take those actions that she thinks will maximize utility. Hence, allocations of commodities cannot be Pareto optimal.

Let us consider the point from another angle. A right to autonomy is also inalienable. A right to autonomy is inalienable in the same respects as Morris's right to be treated as a person in that

(a) it is a right that cannot be transferred to another in the way one's right with respect to objects can be transferred and (b) that it cannot be waived in the ways in which people talk of waiving rights to property . . . (Morris 1976: 53).

However, the basis of the inalienability of a right to autonomy differs from that of a right to be treated as a person. The grounds of the inalienability of a right to be treated as a person lies in personhood, in the implications of the right, and in the meaning of the right. Regarding the inalienability of autonomy, Arthur Kuflik (1984: 468) wrote that "a person who is capable of autonomous moral functioning cannot freely and rationally alienate his autonomy; in effect, there can be no genuinely autonomous decision to abdicate autonomy." A right to autonomy cannot be transferred or waived without undermining normative social practice, because a right to autonomy enables a normative social practice. Since a normative social practice is necessary for efficient outcomes of trade, a right to autonomy is also required for efficiency, though efficiency is not the direct basis of its inalienability. Commodification of anything that involves abrogating one of the moral rights that is a necessary condition of economic efficiency defeats the goal of efficiency. Therefore, there exist logical limits on the commodification of desire.

Summary

We have (1) reiterated that a specified system of normative conditions can secure competitive behavior and, thus, can preclude the effects of intentional externalities, (2) discussed how moral normative constraints and conventions can rectify the effects of intentional and accidental externalities, (3) noted that moral normative constraints converge expectations and thereby reduce transaction costs, and (4) argued that moral normative constraints provide logical limits on the commodification of desire. Without moral normative constraints, externalities cannot be precluded, much less rectified. Without moral normative constraints, expectations will not converge. Without moral normative constraints, there are no limits on the kinds of things that can be commodified. We conclude that a population of strict rational egoists cannot achieve efficient allocations in the absence of moral normative constraints.

6

The Moral Conditions of
Economic Efficiency

I have answered the first central question by establishing that strict rational egoists cannot achieve efficient outcomes of trade in the absence of moral normative constraints. Economic efficiency requires morality. We now turn our attention to the second central question:

> *What are the moral normative constraints and other types of normative conditions of market interaction leading to efficient outcomes?*

In this chapter, I determine and discuss the normative conditions for the achievement of Pareto-optimal equilibrium allocations of commodities.

It is important to note that Pareto-optimal equilibrium allocations of commodities are outcomes of *social* behavior. Analysts have traditionally assumed the consequences of coordinated behavior such as the absence of externalities and competitive behavior. But we have been looking closely at the presuppositions of coordinated behavior. We must not lose sight of the fact that efficient outcomes of trade are outcomes of coordinated social behavior. In this chapter, I specify in detail the elements of a system of social order that coordinates social behavior. In short, I specify the moral conditions of economic efficiency.

Concentrating, as we have, on rules, incentives, and individual behavior can diminish our tacit awareness of the social dimension of trade. Trade is social behavior consisting in a set of exchanges or series of exchanges.[1] A set or series of exchanges that results in efficient outcomes is norm-guided social behavior. Both coordination norms and collective action norms guide a group of agents toward the achievement of Pareto-optimal equilibrium allocations of commodities. I will devote more attention to coordination norms and to collective action norms later; for now I will emphasize that Pareto-optimal equilibrium outcomes of commodities depend on norm-guided social behavior.

We may enhance our appreciation of the norm-guided character of social behavior resulting in efficient allocations of commodities by viewing it in terms of perfect competition and its conditions. An equilibrium allocation is Pareto optimal only if every individual acts perfectly competitively. Individuals act perfectly competitively just in case each is a price-taker, that is, just in case every agent takes (what we have defined as) market actions only. However, I argued in Chapter 3 that perfect competition exists only in and because of a perfectly competitive market. I have shown that a perfectly competitive market is an institution that includes a set of moral normative constraints and a set of conventions for equilibrating supply and demand and for "internalizing" externalities. Every individual's acting perfectly competitively is not accidental or coincidental social behavior but rather norm-guided social behavior. Therefore, every equilibrium allocation is Pareto optimal only if individuals' behavior is guided by norms held in common. The regularity in social behavior guided by such norms is a normative social practice.

Second, the conditions of Pareto-optimal equilibrium allocations of commodities achieved through trade comprise a system of conditions. A simple list of conditions would not be an adequate description of the conditions I am seeking to determine. Describing how efficient allocations of commodities are possible by simply listing the conditions would be much like describing how a small engine functions by looking at a parts list. In both cases, essential relationships between conditions must be described.

The Concept of a Normative Social Practice

In this section, I present the idea of a normative social practice in stages by defining it and by correlating, comparing, and differentiating it from similar concepts. The stages after the definition should not be seen as discussions of analytical elements of the concept of a normative social practice, or as hard-edged claims in social theory. Rather, they should be viewed as conceptual scaffolding intended as temporary aids in the construction of a new concept. When the new concept is adequately grasped and usable, the scaffolding is no longer required.

A *normative social practice* is a social phenomenon – a regularity in social behavior – (1) guided by beliefs held in common (a) concerning the criteria by which a group of individuals evaluate their own and others' behavior and according to which criteria they hold each other responsible and (b) concerning the procedures for holding each other responsible, and (2) the purpose of which is directly pertinent to individuals' well-being, or identity, or sense of community, or some other such thing commonly held in high value.

The social phenomena of norms, conventions, institutions, firms, and legal systems, in addition to customs, mores, laws, and the like, constitute a family of concepts that have been subject to various analyses and debate in recent years.[2] Accounts of these social phenomena are formal in that they involve explications not of any social phenomena in particular, but rather of the form of such phenomena. In other words, theorists who offer such accounts are not doing empirical studies – they are not doing anthropology or sociology – rather, they are engaged in rational reconstruction. Each of these theorist's analysis depends on an hypothetical account of how the social phenomena might emerge. Similarly, I take normative social practice to be a distinct member of this family of social phenomena. As far as I know, there is no extensive, much less widely accepted, analysis of a normative social practice. However, the account I offer is neither an abstraction from actual moralities nor merely an analysis of our concept of morality, nor does my explication involve an account of how it might emerge. Rather I adopt a pattern of rational reconstruction abstracted from the methodology of several different theorists, none of whom offer either purely empirical or purely conceptual analyses.

Let me elaborate on the concept of a normative social practice by correlating it with the concept of an empirical morality. Any particular empirical morality is an instance of a normative social practice. There exist a number of differing empirical moralities, each being a complex set of beliefs and regularities in behavior[3] that differentiate one group of people from others. An empirical morality entails a set of beliefs which I will call a worldview. However, not every empirical morality's constituent worldview is fully developed by its practitioners. A fully developed worldview includes beliefs regarding a conception of the good, a view of human nature, a diagnosis of thwarted ideals, and so on. Principles and procedures governing certain kinds of action are based on these beliefs. Second, an empirical morality is a relatively coherent complex of beliefs and regularities in behavior.[4] Therefore, no account of any particular empirical morality can be given by a mere listing of its characteristic types of beliefs and practices. Beliefs and practices are related in crucial and relatively invariant ways.

Consider the following thought experiment as a heuristic device. Suppose that for some defined, yet fairly substantial, population, all questions of moral philosophy have been settled. They agree, let us suppose, that not giving false information is the one and only correct moral standard of action. That is, an action is morally correct for them if and only if it does not involve the giving of false information. Such a society functions in practice, first of all, by everyone's holding the belief that he or she ought to observe the rule not to give false information. Since everyone's actions are constrained only by the rule, everyone is free to consider alternative courses of action and to assess them by the standard. When anyone takes some action that appears to be morally wrong, there must exist some mechanism by which the offense can be verified, the liability can be relieved, and the offender can be restored to communal membership. This complex and coherent interconnection of belief and regularity in behavior makes an empirical morality a normative social practice.

Empirical moralities may differ not only in their substantive rules and in their underlying worldview but also in their respective regularities in behavior. Yet each involves substantive rules, an underlying worldview, and regularities in behavior. Furthermore, each will involve procedures for holding each other responsible and will involve alternative strategies to relieve liability. For example, in a very clumsy and undeveloped empirical morality, it might be imagined that individuals hold each other responsible by holding grudges and exacting revenge. Individuals in this morality learn to identify facial expressions and demeanors to assess whether others are offended in any way. By contrast, rational confrontation and a greater repertoire of strategies for relieving liability such as compensation and restitution supplemented with forgiveness is a more advanced and a more effective method for promoting a sense of community and peace. The point is that each empirical morality involves some identifiable way of holding each other responsible and of relieving liability. These are invariant and constituent aspects of virtually any empirical morality. A normative social practice, therefore, constitutes an empirical morality's ideal conditions.

We may distinguish a normative social practice from a social practice simpliciter. In one sense, every social practice is "normative" for those engaged in it. The former is guided by collective action norms (though it also might involve coordination norms); the latter is guided only by coordination norms. Social practices simpliciter are regularities in behavior whose coordination rules may or may not be codified. Moreover, the relation of social practices simpliciter to individuals' well-being, identity, or sense of community differs from the relation of normative social practices to those same things. For examples, playing games like "Hide-and Seek," bringing a gift to the host family when invited over for dinner, and Hume's example of two men rowing a boat are examples of social practices simpliciter. The point of each of these practices seems to lack the urgency, depth, or scope that the purposes of normative social practices have. Perhaps, it would be more accurate to say that the values pertinent to each type of practice lie on a continuum such that normative social practices aim to achieve the most highly valued social goals, while social practices simpliciter aim to achieve less-valued social goals.[5]

A normative social practice among a group of people also involves holding one another responsible. It is outside the scope of this book to review the current philosophical discussions on the concept of responsibility.[6] Nevertheless, my use of the notion of holding each other responsible is virtually uncontroversial. To hold someone responsible is to hold that person accountable and liable for his or her behavior. A normative social practice involves the expectation that explanations for actions apparently contrary to established criteria will be provided. To hold someone *accountable* is to require such an explanation. "Successful" explanations of contrary behavior will either justify or excuse the action. If an individual fails to justify or to excuse her actions, she is held *liable*. There are several strategies for relieving liability: restoration, restitution, compensation, punishment, and forgiveness.[7] Thus, holding someone accountable involves holding that person liable absent a justifying explanation. Failing to hold individuals accountable for actions that appear prima facie contrary to established criteria has a deleterious effect on the community holding to the practice.[8] I will refer to this complex set of procedures as the *responsibility schema*.[9]

The general difference between a social practice simpliciter and a normative social practice can be seen by considering hypothetical responses by practitioners to mistakes made by initiates or novices. In a social practice *simpliciter*, an insider might respond to a mistake by explaining, "This just is not the way we do things." There are no judgmental connotations in the comment implying that the individual may not need to do anything to relieve liability for the error. However, given a behavior contrary to a norm constituting a normative social practice, the comment – "that is not the way we do things" – has judgmental implications. It is not that someone merely did something different ("why didn't I think of that" or "I am sorry I did not realize it") or embarrassing, but that someone did something wrong that has serious consequences that require rectification.

Nevertheless, the "edges" of each social phenomenon seem not to be sharp enough to indicate a clearly demarcated distinction. Therefore, we should view normative social practices and social practices simpliciter more like poles of a continuum having areas that fade into each other or areas of overlap.

The concept of a normative social practice differs from Andrew Schotter's (1981) influential notion of a social institution. Schotter's definition of a system of property rights as a social institution exhibits certain inadequacies that are inherent in defining a system of property rights merely as a regularity in behavior and not as a regularity in social behavior guided by a set of rules. More importantly, a conception of property rights as a social institution is not sufficient to make efficient outcomes of trade possible because a social institution is not a normative social practice, therefore, and is not sufficient to secure competitive behavior. Schotter develops his notion of a social institution by reference to Lewis's notion of a convention. David Lewis (1969: 58) defines convention as follows:

A regularity R in the behavior of members of a population P when they are agents in a recurrent situation S is a convention if and only if it is true that, and it is common knowledge in P that, in any instance of S among members of P,
(1) everyone conforms to R;
(2) everyone expects everyone else to conform to R;
(3) everyone prefers to conform to R on condition that the others do, since S is a coordination problem and uniform conformity to R is a coordination equilibrium in S.

Notice that Lewis defines convention in terms of a regularity in behavior. Lewis's examples of conventions are meeting every week at the same place, calling back if disconnected if you are the originating caller, driving in the right lane in the United States, and using the same language if you are a member of a group, among others.

A convention defined by Lewis is virtually identical to a social practice simpliciter. However, the term *convention* is commonly used to refer either to a rule (understood as a linguistic expression of a norm) that governs behavior or to a regularity in behavior itself. Lewis does not explicate how conforming to regularity R relates to conforming one's behavior to a rule. Since Schotter's notion of a social institution depends upon Lewis's convention, the lack of clarity carries over as well. Schotter (1981: 11) defined the concept of a social institution as follows:

A regularity R in the behavior of members of a population P when they are agents in a recurrent situation Γ is an *institution* if and only if it is true that, and it is common knowledge in P that,

(1) everyone conforms to R;

(2) everyone expects everyone else to conform to R;

(3) everyone prefers to conform to R on condition that the others do, if Γ is a coordination problem and uniform conformity to R is a coordination equilibrium in Γ or

(4) if anyone ever deviates from R it is known that some or all of the others will also deviate and the payoffs associated with the recurrent play of Γ using these deviating strategies are worse for all agents than the payoff associated with R.

Conforming to R is simply what everyone does, expects everyone else to do, prefers to do, and knows that all will be worse off by not conforming to R. Conditions (1) through (4) convey no sense of individuals being and feeling obligated in reference to a rule at least believing that everyone *ought* to conform to a rule that prescribes a behavior exemplified by R. If a *social institution* is a social phenomenon guided by commonly held rules, then it requires a distinction between regularities in behavior and the rules that guide those regularities – a distinction that Schotter did not make.

Schotter did not follow Lewis in using gerund phrases to name regularities in behavior. For example, Schotter wrote that "money is a social convention (1981: 3)" instead of using money is a social convention, and that "language" and "table manners" are social conventions (1981: 9) in place of a group's using the same language and *everyone's observing the same rules of etiquette* are social conventions.

These observations illustrate how the term *convention* is used to refer either to a rule, or to a regularity in behavior or to conflate the two. Schotter carried this conflation over to his list of examples of social institutions. He wrote that a "system of property rights is a social institution (p. 11)." Thus, by definition, a system of property rights must be regularity in behavior. But a system of property rights is a set or rules that makes a regularity in social behavior possible.

Contrasting his view with Hurwicz's (1973) account of institutions, Schotter (1981: 61) wrote that "we view social institutions not as various sets of rules but as various and alternative standards of behavior (strategy n-tuples) that are elements of the equilibrium of the game. In other words, our social institutions are not part of the rules of the game but part of the solutions to iterated games of strategy." In more technical terms, whereas Schotter's social institution is a solution to a game, a normative social practice is a "family of game-forms."[10] Viewing institutions as a family of game-forms emphasizes the rules involved in guiding the behavior of individuals, or at least acknowledges the difference between rules and regularities in behavior.

The concept of a normative social practice is richer than Schotter's notion of a social institution. The crucial differences between normative social practice and Schotter's social institution are several. Differing instantiated normative social practices are distinguished by their respective substantive rules. The particular type of normative social practice required for efficient outcomes of trade must include a set of property rights, but also a right to true information and a right to welfare. Schotter indicated that a set of property rights constitutes a social institution and differentiates it from others. However, if a right is a claim against the behavior of others, then a property right (in one very limited sense) is a claim against others' using the object in question. Refraining from using an object is behavior enjoined by the right; it is not the right itself. Hence, a system of property rights cannot logically be identical to the behavior it regulates. Moreover, even though it might seem proper to say that competitive behavior is a regularity in behavior that could be described in terms of everyone observing a set of property rights, it is incomplete at best to say that property rights, construed as a regularity in behavior, constitute the conditions that make efficient trade possible. Certainly, everyone behaves competitively only if everyone respects each other's property rights. But an adequate model will depict competitive behavior in relation to existing rules and agents' beliefs and preference relations. It must represent why agents behave competitively.

Another way to state this difference is in terms introduced by H. L. A. Hart (1994: 89) regarding the internal and external points of view. Hart wrote,

When a social group has certain rules of conduct, this fact affords an opportunity for many closely related yet different kinds of assertion; for it is possible to be concerned with the rules, either merely as an observer who does not himself accept them, or as a member of the group which accepts and uses them as guides to conduct. We may call these respectively the "external" and the "internal points of view."

In our model, each individual is fully aware of each other's rights, not as elements in an analytical model of social interaction, nor as premises in a proof, but as features of the situation in which they act. Each agent, that is, takes an internal point of view regarding his or her behavior. Even though a description of their behavior may be given by an outside observer as respecting each other's property rights, from the internal perspective agents are aware of each other's rights, which are aspects of the conditions of competitive behavior. Therefore, respecting each other's property rights describes some aspects of competitive behavior, but not its conditions.

The concept of a normative social practice offers an analytical understanding of the conditions of agents' behavior, not merely a description, and therefore differs significantly from Schotter's notion of a social institution. The notion of a social institution does not indicate the logical connections between a system of property rights as a regularity in behavior, agents' preferences and incentives, and procedures for holding one another accountable. A social institution is a solution to a coordination game. Since a solution to a game is not a family of game-forms, a social institution perforce omits the rules that constitute both the game and the conditions of its iteration. The concept of a normative social practice makes these connections explicit. Therefore, the idea of a normative social practice must be differentiated from Schotter's notion of a social institution. The idea of a normative social practice succeeds in accounting for the conditions that secure competitive behavior whereas the concept of a social institution fails.

Rights in General

The system of normative conditions of efficient outcomes of trade includes moral normative constraints construed as rights. This is not intended to suggest that all moral normative constraints involve rights. An alternative system of moral normative constraints that instantiates the Moral Principle Solution to collective action problems might be developed. Whether or not my moral rights-based system of normative conditions is more basic than, or weaker than, or even logically related to, say, a Kantian system is not obvious. Moreover, it is beyond the scope of this book to formulate a position on this issue. Nevertheless, my moral rights-based system does seem to be less alien to extant economic, game-form, and social choice models than most, if not all, Moral Principle Solutions. Indeed, in many respects it is already adapted to such models. For example, the framework for analyzing social situations, which we adopted in Chapter 2, is directly related to standard assumptions in microeconomic theory. Rights construed as restrictions of agents' natural strategy domains have already been discussed by game-theorists.[11] And the system of normative conditions presented in this book suggests a solution to Amartya Sen's (1970a, 1970b, 1992) Liberal Paradox, an important result in social choice theory.

In sum, I use rights rather than moral rules or principles for several reasons. First, there is a growing literature in economics and social choice theory that uses the concept of a right formally to depict restrictions on agents' natural strategy domains.[12] The concept of a right is also used because the system of normative conditions I am proposing is essentially an economic system, and I desire as much as possible that my model observe the existing formal models and conventions of economics and social choice theory. Second, the rights I adduce are compatible with a wide range of moral traditions. Therefore, the system of normative conditions could be applicable in pluralistic democracies, which, by definition, encompass diverse moral perspectives. Last, there is an empirical study showing that altruistic behavior, which crosses normal boundaries of ethnicity, is motivated in part by virtue of a recognition of others' rights – even though the content of the rights believed to be binding vary somewhat between altruists.[13] Since the rights I offer are applicable in a range of differing moral settings, their compatibility with this account of altruistic motivation is an asset.

A right is one aspect of one type of normative constraint. In this section, I offer a conception of a right as one of two essential aspects of a moral normative constraint suitable for economic modeling. I am not attempting to analyze the concept of a right as it is commonly used, nor am I attempting to correct common usage. Recall from Chapter 1 that, generally speaking, a *constraint* is some device that inhibits the occurrence of some types of actions, and there are at least two kinds of constraints – positive and normative. An individual's budget constraint and information constraints are examples of positive constraints. These delimit an individual's natural strategy domain. Normative constraints restrict individuals' natural strategy domains and thus delimit agents' admissible strategy domains. Normative constraints constitute a broad subclass of constraints including legal, moral, institutional, and organizational constraints (i.e., all nonpositive constraints).

Since we are focusing on a type of normative constraint constituted by a right and by an incentive for compliance with that right, we must show how it functions as an aspect of a normative constraint. Since a right is only one aspect of a normative constraint, it is not precise to say that a right restricts an individual's natural strategy domain. A right is correlated with a rule, which expresses the content of a standard against which individuals assess each other's behavior including their own. An incentive to comply with rules constitutes the other aspect of a restriction on an individual's natural strategy domain. We discuss incentive to comply later. As a rough approximation, we may consider a *right* to be a certain kind of claim correlated with a rule. We may then say that

A person i is *normatively constrained* by a right when some other person j has a claim against i regarding some type of action A and i has an incentive to comply with the rule correlated with the claim.

We must be able to associate rights with duties, liberties, and the like, to express accurately just how agents' natural strategy domains are restricted. I accomplish this by adopting Wesley N. Hohfeld's (1919) analysis of rights. Hohfeld's analyzes fundamental legal concepts in a way that to this day is generally considered by scholars to be nearly definitive[14] and is essential to a more finely grained portrayal of rights.[15]

To define a right so that it expresses a restriction on agents' natural strategy domains requires that it be defined in terms of actions, not social states. However, some Hohfeldian analyses of rights are presented in terms of social states. For example, in a series of articles, Stig Kanger develops Hohfeld's analysis and defines rights in terms of social states. We may state Kanger's conception of a claim as follows:

> For any two agents *i and j,* and any states of affairs $\sigma_n(i, j)$ involving both agents *i* and *j*, *i* has versus *j* a *claim* regarding $\sigma_n(i, j)$ if and only if *j* has a duty to bring about $\sigma_n(i, j)$.

I am neither endorsing nor criticizing Kanger's analysis here. I am simply citing an example of a Hohfeldian analysis that defines rights in terms of social states. By contrast, in my model, rights are elements of normative constraints and should therefore be conceived in terms of individuals' actions. Thus, I define a claim and a liberty (privilege) as follows:

Claim. A person *i* has a *claim* against person *j* with respect to some action if and only if *j* has a duty to *i* to perform that action.

For example, if *j* has a duty to *i* to provide true information, then person *i* has a claim against person *j* with respect to *j*'s provision of information.

Liberty. A person *i* has a *liberty* against person *j* to perform some action *A* if and only if *i* has no duty to *j* not to perform *A*.

For example, if *i* has no duty to *j* not to paint her house white, then *i* has a liberty against person *j* to modify her property as she pleases, which, in this case, is to paint it white.

Correlatives apply to persons other than the element-holder, and there is a two-way entailment between elements and correlatives. For each right held by some individual, at least one other individual has a correlative duty. Although there are exceptions, in this book each right is correlated with some duty held by others by virtue of the social goal of achieving efficient outcomes of trade. Of course, there are cases in which someone may have a duty, but for which no one has a claim right; and, in these cases, a moral claim right cannot be characterized in terms of a biconditional. Nevertheless, the biconditional applies to all the moral rights I name. The same holds for a Hohfeldian liberty. In a very general sense, a right constitutes one aspect of a restriction on an individual's natural strategy domain. But since a right is a claim against others with respect to some action, it is more precise to say that a right expresses the extent to which some other individual's natural strategy domain is restricted. In a later section, I specify a set of rights, each of which is defined as a set of Hohfeldian positions.

There are two competing conceptualizations of rights in economic analysis – social choice and game-form. A social choice conceptualization of a right treats a right as a desideratum of a social decision mechanism, implying that the right – or what the right protects – is intrinsically valued. Even though an equilibrium allocation is a social state achieved by an aggregation of individual decisions, and, therefore, the system of moral normative constraints I develop is a social decision mechanism, a right in my model is not best thought of as a desideratum of such mechanisms (although a right plays an essential part in the function of a social decision mechanism). Thus, rights can be viewed primarily in terms of their instrumental value since they form an essential aspect of a condition of efficient outcomes of trade. However, this is not to imply that rights could not also be valued for themselves or for what they protect in addition to their instrumental function. Indeed, the effectiveness of rights in securing competitive behavior (and thereby efficient outcomes of trade) may be strengthened by individuals valuing the observation of rights for their own sake or valuing the role of rights in sustaining character attributes.

My goal is to specify a minimal system of normative conditions that make efficient outcomes of trade possible, not to review alternative accounts of their value nor to explore their social implications. I have already argued for a construal of rights as restricting agents' natural strategy domains, and I will offer two alternative ways to model an internally based motive to comply with rights. Therefore, I need not extend this discussion of rights to include investigations into their being intrinsically valued or valued for what they protect. Furthermore, the intrinsic/instrumental distinction with respect to rights would at least need to be investigated in connection with a discussion of existing philosophical theories of rights, which is a discussion beyond the scope of this book.[16] For our immediate purpose, it is important to mention only that no philosophical theory entails a denial that an essential feature of the concept of a right involves a constraint on other's actions, thereby enabling the achievement of efficient allocations of commodities.[17]

A *game-form* conceptualization of a right, on the other hand, depicts a right as a restriction on agents' natural strategy domains. My analysis requires that I conceive a right primarily as it relates to agents' actions, and as only indirectly relating to social states. Since I construe rights to express specific restrictions on agents' natural strategy domains, I adopt the game-form conceptualization of rights.

The rights I adduce are moral rights. There are several reasons why the system of rights I specify should be understood as a system of *moral* rights.[18] First, given what these rights can be understood to accomplish (i.e., to reduce waste, promote well-being, and foster communal harmony), it is difficult to conceive of them as not being moral in some sense of the term. Second, we could summarize the debates concerning a rule of recognition for morality and argue that the system I specify meets the correct conditions.[19] But the strength of that claim rests on the strength of the arguments for some rule of recognition. Such a discussion is beyond the scope of this book.[20] Third, the rights I adduce could be considered to be moral rights on the grounds of several alternative moral theories such as rule utilitarianism, natural rights theory, or on a conception of agents. A rule utilitarian could argue that the rights are moral because they maximize total welfare.[21] A natural rights theorist could argue that the rights are moral because they derive from a conception of agents as project-pursuers. Some philosophers ground moral rights in the purposive action of agents.[22] As James Coleman (1990: 17) wrote,

In a certain range of scholarly endeavor, including ethics, moral philosophy, political philosophy, economics, and law, theory is based on an image of man as a purposive and responsible actor.

Tara Smith (1995: 32) wrote,

My contention is that respect for individual rights to freedom of action is a necessary condition for individuals' attainment of their highest good. Each person's own life is that person's ultimate value. It can only be attained, though, when a person is free to rule her own life. If we wish to have the chance to achieve that value, then we must respect rights.

Rawls (1971: 408) followed Josiah Royce in viewing an individual as "a human life lived according to a plan." Rights protect individuals' freedoms to pursue their projects. It seems that such a conception of rights fits well with my project. However, I want to avoid the debates concerning the proper or best conception of human agents, which accompany such theories.[23] So I do not attempt to ground such rights in the purposive action of agents. Fourth, since we have excluded the existence of a state, we might conceive such rights as having been instituted by mutual consent. The rights I adduce are either substantive – being instituted by consent – or constitutive of a (certain kind) of normative social practice.[24] Substantive rights have moral relevance by virtue of their grounding in consent.[25] By these comments I do not mean to suggest that all rights instituted by consent are full-fledged moral rights. I intend only to suggest how a contractarian moral theorist could argue that the system of rights adduced here could be construed as the object of an hypothetical social contract.

Finally, I do not attempt to ground rights in moral principles or the "principles of enlightened conscience" (as Feinberg put it), though one of the rights expresses a rule of autonomy that enables a normative social practice to exist. It is presupposed by morality insofar as it is a practice. The other rights I adduce are substantive, and, therefore, the system can serve itself as a simple code for an empirical morality. Thus, although it is possible to argue on several alternative grounds that the rights in this system are moral, because this system is intended only to be adequate for efficient trade, the rights included in it are intended to be moral in a minimal, yet widely applicable sense.

To each type of action that threatens to preclude the achievement of efficiency, there corresponds a proscriptive or prescriptive rule. The corresponding rule could be expressed like this: Do not give false information that is directly pertinent to potential exchange. Each rule can be correlated with a right defined in terms of some set of "Hohfeldian positions." For example, the rule not to give false information that is directly pertinent to potential exchange can be correlated with a right to true information (pertinent to potential exchange), which in turn can better be expressed in the following form of a moral Hohfeldian position:

A person i has a claim-right against person j to provide true information (pertinent to potential exchange) if and only if j has a duty to i to provide true information (which is directly pertinent to potential exchange).

What distinguishes these moral Hohfeldian positions from legal Hohfeldian positions is their bases for validating claims and the type of incentive required for compliance: moral normative constraints include sufficient internal incentives to comply, whereas legal normative constraints do not. These moral Hohfeldian positions are grounded either in consent or in the nature of a normative social practice. Furthermore, these moral Hohfeldian positions express restrictions on individuals' natural strategy domains, but only when combined with sufficient internal incentives to comply do they comprise moral normative constraints.

Compliance

In this section, I discuss the compliance problem and alternative ways to model the *Agents* subset so as to achieve a motive to comply with existing rules. However, I must add this caveat: The crucial result so far is that, for strict rational egoists, no external enforcement mechanism will secure the requisite behavior needed for efficient trade. Individuals must have *some* moral motivation independent of any external sanctions that may exist. It is beyond the scope of this book to determine which moral motivations are superior in this regard, and it is not necessary to describe any particular one in detail. Some moral conditions of Pareto-optimal equilibrium allocations can be given by specifying a set of rights and procedures and a range of alternative moral motivations, any one of which can create an incentive for compliance.

To present the compliance problem with sufficient clarity, consider first an alternative construal of the argument presented thus far. There is a difference between the extent of welfare loss in social states brought about by acts of theft in situations on the one hand, and the extent of welfare loss in social states caused by *the moral possibility of theft* in a society, or the physical possibility of accidents, negligence, and the like on the other hand. Recall that strict rational egoists will invariably act according to this principle:

(DPA) For any person i, action a_n^i, and state of affairs σ_n, i will take a_n^i if and only if i prefers σ_n and i has good reason to believe that a_n^i is the best feasible means to achieve σ_n.

Therefore, if by taking some nonmarket action (i.e., by engaging in noncompetitive behavior) an individual can more efficiently achieve her goal social state, she will take that nonmarket action and will effect some Pareto-inferior social state. Similar welfare loss results from accidents, negligence, and the like. These are the consequences of the actions of a single individual. For a population of strict rational egoists, by contrast, nonmarket action (e.g., theft or fraud) is always morally possible. In a society in which such nonmarket actions are morally possible, labor resources are wasted by forgoing commodity production in favor either of engaging in nonmarket actions or of defending against them. Thus, rational self-interest in such a society inexorably leads to suboptimal equilibrium allocations of resources. Everyone would be better off by behaving competitively. Furthermore, where no means exist to redress harm caused by negligence or accidents, there is a similar loss of welfare. Strict rational egoists will behave competitively and take proper care only if they face some system of moral normative constraints that renders nonmarket actions undesirable, thereby inhibiting their occurrence, and that provides a set of procedures for rectifying the harmful results of any particular nonmarket action. Some set of procedures is required to establish liability and to relieve liability for any transgressions. Without such a system, welfare loss from deliberate or unintentional transgression would lead rational egoists to consider courses of action to recover losses from such actions or to devote resources to guard against such losses in amounts over which might be warranted even when such a system is in place.

We model a moral normative constraint as a moral right, which indicates a restriction on an individual's natural strategy domain and defines an admissible strategy domain. However, a set of moral rights by itself is not sufficient to secure competitive behavior. Strict rational egoists will achieve Pareto-optimal equilibrium allocations only by agreeing on the required rights and by complying with them. Thus, a right is only one aspect of a moral normative constraint. An incentive for compliance is the other. An individual, therefore, is moral normatively constrained if she has a sufficient internal incentive to observe others' rights that restrict her natural strategy domain. In this sense, a moral normative constraint is constituted by a right and an incentive.

In Chapter 3, I showed that strict rational egoists will always have an incentive to free-ride on the obligation to enforce a rule regardless of whether the enforcement mechanism is centralized or decentralized. The Hobbesian solution to collective action problems involves the creation of *Leviathan,* which is a centralized mechanism to enforce property rights. Since the Hobbesian solution is a centralized solution, there is always the possibility that the enforcers will have an incentive to take nonmarket actions to advance their own interests. So, both rules and an enforcement mechanism are needed for the enforcers. This leads to an infinite regress of enforcer classes. A decentralized enforcement mechanism, on the other hand, involves everyone in enforcing claims.[26] However, even a decentralized enforcement mechanism among a population of strict rational egoists will fail because individuals will have an incentive to let others expend the resources required to hold an offender responsible. Therefore, compliance is not possible for strict rational egoists. This, then, is the compliance problem: Even if strict rational egoists agree in principle on a set of rights, they will not observe them or fulfill an obligation to enforce them. Compliance is a matter of motivation. Since strict rational egoists are completely unaffected by moral considerations of any kind, to secure compliance we must alter the *Agent* subset of assumptions.

Before we go on, perhaps we should pause and briefly summarize what we have before us to hold each of the elements of the argument in place. In Chapter 3, we showed that strict rational egoists cannot achieve Pareto-optimal equilibrium allocations of commodities through trade. Therefore, both the *Situation* subset and the *Agent* subset of assumptions must be altered. Introducing rules into the *Situation* subset is insufficient by itself because rules by themselves are not normative constraints. Individuals subjectively experience a normative constraint as an effective restriction on the range of actions they are physically able to take. Viewed objectively, however, a normative constraint is an enforced rule. Therefore, we must furnish some means to enforce whatever rules are introduced. However, an enforcement mechanism cannot be built into the *Situation* subset because, since such an enforcement mechanism would have to be construed as a universal obligation to hold everyone else responsible and to punish defectors, everyone will have an incentive to free-ride. Hence, by altering the *Situation* subset alone, we cannot construct a normative constraint; altering the *Situation* subset alone is not sufficient.

Consider the following, which sets the compliance problem in stark relief and suggests some minimum requirements. Matthews (1981) offers an argument for the effectiveness of honesty and trust. However, trust involves the expectation that the person with whom one dealing is honest. If honesty entails "telling the truth," then honesty could be construed weakly as a behavior that recognizes and observes others' right to true information.[27] Unlike most violations of property rights, a violation of another's right to true information is difficult to detect, except after the fact. For a right to true information to function as a moral normative constraint, individuals must be able to detect violations.

Since detection is not always possible, individuals must have some kind of internal motivation for compliance (with the rules, not simply with the obligation to enforce them), even when such compliance may not maximize utility in the short term. But strict rational egoists do not possess the requisite motivation.

In sum, strict rational egoists do not possess the requisite motivation to comply with the rights they agree on, even though it is collectively rational to do so. To get compliance, we must therefore alter our depiction of individuals, construing them as subject to other motives besides maximization of utility narrowly defined. To put it another way, the strict rational egoist assumption must be altered so that the agents in question will rationally expend resources to sustain a type of society in which their interests are satisfied. In other words, we must "build into" individuals a set of values that at least compete with self-interest narrowly defined. If such values are internalized and are seen to be logically connected to moral rights as ends to means, both aspects of a moral normative constraint will be in place. Individuals will be aware of specific ways in which their respective natural strategy domains are restricted and will comply as a matter of individual choice based on the strength of alternative values or reasons. This is not to suggest that someone may not internalize the value of observing others' rights for reasons other than efficient outcomes of trade. Everyone's observing others' rights for the intrinsic value of doing so will also result in efficiency. Therefore, viewing the observance of rights instrumentally is not a necessary condition of efficiency. However, an instrumental view of the observance of rights is "weaker" than an intrinsic view, and, since the instrumental view does not rule out the intrinsic view, the instrumental view is to be desired by virtue of our goal of obtaining a "weak" but adequate conception of a system of moral normative constraints specified sufficiently to depict the achievement of efficient trade among rational egoists. Regardless, efficient outcomes of trade require not only rules but also motives that provide sufficient incentives to comply with the rules. We must, therefore, alter both subsets of assumptions in the framework for analyzing social situations, which we introduced in Chapter 2.

We have briefly discussed five ways to model internal motivation for compliance while retaining self-interest. In Chapter 2, we ruled out the possibility that agents' preferences might range over alternative visions of society as a whole, character types, or decision rules. Preferences could range over others' attitudes such as approval or disapproval. And finally, preferences might range over the relative satisfaction of others' preferences. Individuals, that is, can have altruistic, sadistic, or merely meddlesome preferences.

I will discuss just two of these alternatives.[28] First of all, consider the possibility of agents' preferences ranging over alternative character descriptions. The variations seem countless. But suppose each individual has a desire to sustain a certain kind of moral character defined in terms of the observance of a set of universal rights. Notice that an individual's preference provides an incentive to observe that set of rights due to the logical connection between compliance with that set of rights and the maintenance of character defined by the observance of that set of rights. Since they are universal, she holds them against others as well and will be rationally compelled to uphold them if necessary. This alternative institutes the moral principle solution to collective action situations described in Chapter 4. If *every* agent is construed as having this character preference and every agent is a participant in a normative social practice defined by the three substantive rights, efficient trade is made possible because every individual has an incentive to comply.

According to the dual utility solution, agents have both private (egoistic) and social preferences. There seem to be at least two types of social preferences: altruistic preferences and preference for a sense of belonging and community rather than status. We might say that an individual has altruistic preferences if her utility satisfaction is directly related to others' success at maximizing utility or experience of harm: the greater success others have, the higher her utility satisfaction; the greater the intensity or duration of harm that others experience, the lower her utility satisfaction. One may also have a preference for a sense of belonging and community rather than status. To the extent that satisfying one's altruistic preferences or achieving a sense of belonging or community depends upon according one another a set of basic rights, there exists an incentive to observe that set of rights due to the instrumental function of compliance to the well-being of others, to the security of one's membership in a community, and to the maintenance of community itself. An individual forgoes a utility-maximizing strategy if and only if her social preference overrides her private preferences.[29] If those rights include the system of moral normative constraints I discuss here, then agents having this kind of dual utility function can achieve efficient outcomes from trade. In other words, if *every* agent has this dual utility function (differentiated only by irrelevant differences in preferences for commodities), then efficient trade is made possible because every individual has an incentive to comply.

These alternative instantiations of the moral principle solution and the dual utility solution require substantial revision of the idea of strict rational egoism. The dual utility solution requires that we abandon assumption (p_1). The moral principle solution requires that we abandon premises (p_1) and (p_6). Assumption (p_1) stipulates that agents' desires are independent and entails that there exist no internally motivated, morally significant effects on their actions. Of course, such revision would make the agents in our model more like human beings. Most human beings are motivated either by moral principle or by others' attitudes, pain, or well-being. And most human beings participate in some empirical morality.

As I indicated in the introduction, it is not necessary to determine the best way to model agents to provide an incentive to comply with other's rights. I need only offer a plausible construal of such agents. I have given two alternative ways to model an internally based motive to comply; they also seem to have empirical support. I will refer to such agents as responsible altruists only to distinguish them from strict rational egoists.

The Specific Moral Rights Required for Efficient Trade

We are now ready to list a set of specific moral rights that make efficient outcomes of trade possible. Let me describe briefly a pattern according to which the necessity of each right can be justified as part of a system of normative conditions sufficient to ensure efficient outcomes of trade. First of all, distinguish between a description of a type of action and a rule that expresses either its proscription or its prescription. There are several types of action, each of which could be shown either (a) to inevitably cause inefficiency or (b) to be necessary for efficiency. For each action in the list, we could show under which conditions it is a best alternative for rational egoists and cite a corresponding proscription or prescription. Finally, we could refine each rule in terms of Hohfeldian positions and correlate it with a moral right.

Property Rights

Property rights are required for efficient outcomes of market interaction. Dan Usher (1992: 77–89) shows that income distribution under orderly anarchy is Pareto superior to Hobbesian anarchy because efforts that previously had been expended in taking from others are precluded by well-defined and enforced property rights. I have sketched an explanation of how to incorporate such constraints into a model of social interaction by a conception of rights as restrictions on agents' natural strategy domains. Usher does not specify which rights are necessary or how they are enforced. In fact, most discussions of the First Welfare Theorem mention either that individuals have ownership rights or that property rights are well-defined, but few describe in any more detail what they mean. It is outside the scope of this book to review the significant issues in a theory of property. My goal is to state, in terms that constrain individuals' actions, the minimal description of the rights individuals have. Munzer (1990: 17) defined property "both as things (the popular conception) and as relationship between people with respect to things (the sophisticated conception) – provided the context makes clear which conception is meant." For the sake of clarity, I define property as a relationship between individuals with respect to recognized commodities. Therefore to define property rights is to define features of the relationships between people. A. M. Honoré (1961) gave an analysis of the concept of ownership that is widely recognized. Lawrence Becker (1980: 190) modified Honoré's analysis in Hohfeldian terms and claimed that his synthesis is "an adequate tool for analyzing every description of ownership I have come across, from tribal life through feudal society to modern industrial states." There are thirteen elements in Becker's Hohfeldian modification[30] of Honoré's analysis of ownership:

(1) *The right (claim) to possess* – that is, to exclusive physical control of the thing. Where the thing is noncorporeal, possession may be understood metaphorically.

(2) *The right (liberty) to use* – that is, to personal enjoyment of the benefits of the thing (other than those of management and income).

(3) *The right (power) to manage* – that is, to decide how and by whom a thing shall be used.

(4) *The right (claim) to the income* – that is, to the benefits derived from forgoing personal use of a thing, and allowing others to use it.

(5) *The right (liberty) to consume or destroy* – that is, to annihilate the thing.

(6) *The right (liberty) to modify* – that is, to effect changes less extensive than annihilation.

(7) *The right (power) to alienate* – that is, to carry out inter vivos transfers by exchange or gift and to abandon ownership.

(8) *The right (power) to transmit* – that is, to devise or to bequeath the thing.

(9) *The right (claim) to security* – that is, to immunity from expropriation.

(10) *The absence of term* – that is, the indeterminate length of one's ownership rights.

(11) *The prohibition of harmful use* – that is, one's duty to forbear from using the thing in ways harmful to oneself or others.

(12) *Liability to execution* – that is, liability to having the thing taken away as payment for a debt.

(13) *Residuary rules* – that is, the rules governing the reversion of another, if any, of ownership rights that have expired or been abandoned.

The last four elements are not rights even though they are elements of the concept of ownership. Any combination of elements (1)–(8) (i.e., possession, use, management, income, consumption or destruction, modification, alienation, and transmission) in conjunction with element (9), security, represents a variety of ownership. The concept of full ownership is the "concatenation of all the elements."[31]

A Right to True Information

A right to true information is required to preclude fraud and is required for efficient outcomes of market interaction. Therefore, I have been using the term *right to true information that is directly pertinent to potential exchange*. Henceforth, whenever I use the term, *right to true information,* I intend it to be understood as having this condition attached. Regarding fraud, Karni (1989) wrote,

An agent is said to have committed fraud when he misrepresents the information he has at his disposal so as to persuade another individual (principal) to choose a course of action he would not have chosen had he been properly informed. The essential element of this phenomenon is the presence of two individuals both of whom have something to gain from co-operating with each other but who have conflicting interests and differential information.

It is well known that asymmetrically distributed information makes fraud possible by creating the appropriate incentives.

As we mentioned in Chapter 3, Hurwicz (1972) showed that in classical environments individuals have an incentive to misrepresent their willingness to pay to control prices. An individual can accomplish this by calculating a false *offer curve* (which is a false demand curve) such that when combined with others' offer curves, yields that equilibrium price-ratio that would have resulted if the individual had been a monopsonist. He then calculated a set of preferences that correspond to his offer curve and acted accordingly. Thus, he made it appear as though he is price-taking when he is not. The resulting equilibrium allocation is not Pareto optimal. Since this strategy best achieves a goal social state, the individual will take it. Hurwicz further showed that in classical economic environments with numerous, yet finitely many participants, there is no allocation mechanism having a no-trade option that is incentive compatible.

Since even responsible altruists will be faced with an incentive to defraud when information is asymmetrically distributed and fraud is implicitly permitted, competitive behavior requires that each individual hold a right to true information:

A person i has a claim-right against person j to provide true information if and only if j has a duty to i to provide true information.

A Right to Welfare

A right to welfare is required for efficient outcomes of market interaction. As a moral Hohfeldian position, we may define a *right to welfare* as follows:

A person i has a claim-right against every individual j for a portion of their commodities when i's capacity to produce and trade is diminished due to an accident that prevents i's from achieving a subsistence level of welfare if and only if every individual j has a duty to i to transfer a portion his or her wealth under such conditions.

An individual's *admissible consumption set* is a set of consumption bundles each of which are adequate for subsistence. For any allocation outside an individual's admissible consumption set, that agent has an incentive to take nonmarket actions to acquire whatever commodities are necessary for subsistence. Even though in our theoretical model no individual person will intentionally trade herself into poverty, I have not ruled out the possibility of injury due to accidents of nature that could restrict some agent's ability to engage in economic activity. Thus, when such restrictions of economic power are realized, unless individuals can expect that lump-sum transfers will be made from others to themselves ensuring them a subsistence level of income, given the derived principle for action, individuals will not behave competitively. The Second Fundamental Theorem of Welfare Economics shows that any Pareto-optimal equilibrium allocation of commodities can be achieved by the appropriate transfers.

An argument for a right to welfare differs from the arguments supporting other rights. Other rights derive from the goal of efficiency, the two sets of assumptions, and the derived principle for action. In addition to these bases, a right to welfare derives from the *possibility* of an allocation not being within an individual's consumption set. If we modify strict rational egoists so as to possess some sufficient internal incentive to comply with moral rights, we could alter (DPA*) in terms of expected utility theory and get the needed result. Nevertheless, a cumulative case for a right to welfare can be made by supplementing this argument with others. In this analysis, a right to welfare is a right to an allocation of commodities within one's admissible consumption set and is therefore weaker than other conceptions of a right to welfare. I have argued that individuals have a right to welfare based on the social goal of efficiency.[32]

Rational agents who also possess an incentive to comply with the rights required for economic efficiency have at least one reason to institute a right to welfare. Each individual faces two alternatives regarding the probability of debilitating accidents that render their victims unable to sustain a subsistence level of income. Individuals either must perpetually expend resources defending against the possibility of being defrauded or of having their property stolen, or they must perpetually contribute a proportion of their income to sustain the needy. If the expected costs (tangible and intangible) of sustaining the needy (which will include a public system of taxation and welfare administration of some sort) are less than the expected costs of defense or less than the likely amount of direct loss due to theft or fraud or perhaps even less costly than the stress of anxiety regarding their being accident victims or crime victims themselves, they will prefer a society in which a right to welfare exists. Individuals are not concerned solely with achieving a single, one-time allocation of commodities. Rather, they are concerned with sustaining conditions that enable the continual achievement of efficient trade.

In sum, there are two reasons that a right to welfare is a necessary condition of efficient outcomes of trade. First, in situations where even agents who possess internal incentives to comply with morality become accident victims, unless individuals can expect that lump-sum transfers will be made from others to themselves ensuring them a subsistence level of income, they will not behave competitively; they will have incentives to take any action necessary at least to sustain a subsistence level of well-being. Second, since the expected costs (tangible and intangible) of living in social circumstances in which a share of accident victims' needs is provided by others will be less than the expected costs of living in social circumstances in which individuals must devote resources to defend against the possibility of their being accident victims or crime victims themselves, then rationality requires a right to welfare.

A Right to Autonomy

A right to autonomy is required for efficient outcomes of market interaction. Efficient allocations of commodities are possible only if individuals can take purposive action. Purposive action is possible only if each individual is treated as an agent (i.e., only if her actions are not commanded by another). An individual is treated as an agent when she is permitted to choose ends and courses of actions to achieve those ends and when others' responses to individuals are responses to her choices.[33] A normative social practice presupposes that each agent knows what types of actions are proscribed or prescribed and knows the consequences of violation and that each individual implicitly agrees both to guide her actions accordingly and to hold others accountable. Therefore, a *right to autonomy* is a right to guide one's own actions within a circumscribed set of morally possible actions. It also enables a moral normative social practice (a morality) to exist.

Morris (1976: 32) referred to essentially the same concept as a right to be treated as a person. He claims that a right to be treated as a person is natural, inalienable, and absolute. A right to be treated as a person is "natural" because

First, it is a right we have apart from any voluntary agreement into which we have entered. Second, it is not a right that derives from some defined position or status. Third, it is equally apparent that one has the right regardless of the society or community of which one is a member. Finally, it is a right linked to certain features of a class of beings (Morris 1976: 50).

Although a right to autonomy functions identically to a right to be treated as a person, it differs in that it makes no reference to persons, but only to agents. There is more involved in a concept of a person than is involved in the concept of an agent that we have so far. Agents are aspects of persons and, therefore, a *right to autonomy* applies to persons *as agents*. Therefore, although a right to autonomy could be considered a natural right because there is no obvious reason why it could not depend on the bases Morris listed, it depends solely on the concept of a normative social practice, which in turn is a necessary condition of competitive behavior. A right to autonomy, then, is a right to be treated as an agent and is necessary because competitive behavior requires a normative social practice and a right to autonomy enables a normative social practice to exist.

Liberty

Liberty (or freedom) is an important concept often mentioned in connection with market interaction. How do liberty and freedom fit with the conditions of efficiency thus far discussed? Every agent must be free to produce and to trade. Suppose that, for some population of individuals, some subset M of people are permitted to own property, but not in the full Hohfeld–Honoré sense.[34] Members of M voluntarily submit to the restrictions on their liberty. Suppose also that they prefer some consumption bundle to one that they now own and would engage in trade were they free to do so. The preferences of members of the complement of M count for more than those of members of M. Thus, some Pareto-superior allocations are blocked by the moral framework within which trade occurs, even though theft and fraud are absent. Hence, only preventing theft and fraud is not sufficient to secure efficiency. Liberty of action is a necessary condition of efficient outcomes of trade. However, liberty is a vague concept. It is often used to refer to the equally vague concept of a "protected sphere of action." Mill (1848: bk 5, ch 11, sec 2) writes, "Whatever theory we adopt respecting the foundation of the social union, and under whatever political institutions we live, there is a circle around every human being which no government, be it that of one, of a few, or of the many, ought to be permitted to overstep." Hayek (1960: 139) wrote that "Since coercion is the control of the essential data of an individual's action by another, it can be prevented only by enabling the individual to secure for himself some *private sphere where he is protected* [emphasis added] against such interference."[35] Liberty, as envisioned for example by Thomas Jefferson, is a 'cluster right' whose arena of applicability is political. It is much richer and not nearly as basic as the liberty required for efficient trade. However, the question remains as to the precise definition of agents' liberty in my model. An adequate definition must include liberty to produce, use, exchange, and dispose of property. In my model, an agent's liberty to do so is defined by her right to autonomy and every adequately defined Hohfeldian liberty with respect to each commodity. In other words, in my model an agent's "sphere of protected activity" is fully defined by her right to autonomy and her property rights.

A Synopsis of a System of Normative Conditions of Efficient Outcomes of Market Interaction

The system of conditions that make efficient outcomes of trade possible is constituted as follows. Efficient allocations of commodities require a normative social practice whose substantive rules are sets of property rights for each commodity, a right to true information, and a right to welfare. A normative social practice itself entails a right to autonomy and a responsibility schema. A right to autonomy is a constitutive or enabling rule: Unless each individual holds and grants to others a right to autonomy – a right, that is, to guide his or her behavior by commonly held norms – there can be no normative social practice per se. A right to autonomy is, therefore, indirectly necessary for efficient outcomes of trade. Efficient outcomes of trade also require a sufficient incentive to comply with established rules. In addition to this system of moral normative constraints, Pareto-optimal equilibrium allocations also require a set of conventions (such as is modeled by a Walrasian auctioneer) for facilitating exchange and for coordinating supply and demand and for introducing new commodities into market interaction. Finally, the procedures for internalizing externalities include conventions and normative constraints.

A summary of the conditions of Pareto-optimal equilibrium allocations can be represented symbolically as follows:

Pareto-optimal equilibrium allocations result from market interaction ⇔

(1) Agents behave competitively ⇒ [system of moral normative constraints]
(2) Agents observe price conventions ⇒ [price conventions]
(3) Agents observe procedures for internalizing externalities ⇒ [conventions and normative constraints]

In other words, a system of moral normative constraints, *conventions* for equilibrating supply and demand, and conventions and normative constraints for internalizing externalities are the background presuppositions of the First Fundamental Theorem of Welfare economics:

Every equilibrium allocation is Pareto optimal if and only if
(1) There exists a normative social practice such that
    (i) Property rights for each commodity, a right to true information, a right to welfare, and a right to autonomy are held by each agent, and
    (ii) Each agent has some sufficient internal incentive to comply with these rights, and
    (iii) There exists some responsibility schema, and
(2) There exists some set of price conventions, and
(3) There exist conventions and normative constraints for commodifying desire and for rectifying the results of accidental and intentional externalities.[36]

These are the moral conditions of economic efficiency.[37]

7

Implications

We have addressed two central questions regarding the moral conditions of economic efficiency. We answered the first question by establishing that a population of strict rational egoists *cannot* achieve efficient allocations of commodities through market interaction in the absence of moral normative constraints. We answered the second question by specifying a system of moral normative conditions, which is necessary and sufficient for economic efficiency.

Clarifying the role of moral normative constraints in the achievement of economically efficient outcomes of trade required a refinement of concepts and rigorous analytical tools. In this chapter, I first briefly review and discuss these concepts and analytical tools. I then focus on some results of this analysis that are important for economics, legal theory, political theory, and moral philosophy.

Concepts and Analytical Tools

Normative Social Practice

I use the term *normative social practice* to elucidate the concept of morality as a social phenomenon. This allows us to distinguish its referent from the referents of cognates like David Lewis's *convention* and Andrew Schotter's *social institution*. Moreover, the concept is heuristically valuable for moral philosophy and for research involving ethical considerations.

Right to Autonomy

A right to autonomy is a necessary condition of normative social practices and is a moral right. This concept avoids some of the ambiguity of related terms such as *freedom, liberty, and autonomy,* thus providing more precision in the analysis of legal, moral, political, and economic questions that trade in such concepts. The argument in Chapter 5, that a right to autonomy places a logical limit on the kinds of things that can be turned into commodities, has practical application for public policy formation and for judicial decisions at the appellate level regarding the proper assignment of property rights. I discuss the second aspect of this claim in the next section.

Framework for Analyzing Social Situations

The framework for analyzing social situations can be used to model a wide range of alternative social situations in addition to the types I have modeled in this analysis. Various alternative configurations of agents' attributes, information, and constraints can be modeled. Furthermore, the framework can be converted into a mathematical model, as I did in Chapter 3, where agents are portrayed as having the information-processing capabilities of a Turing Machine and as possessing perfect information regarding every economically relevant variable. Alternative configurations of rights can be modeled as alternative sets of restrictions on agents' natural strategy domains. Thus, the framework can be used to model mathematically both actual types of situations and prospective sets of rights so as to predict possible ranges of outcomes of social interaction. This suggests that further research could refine this model so that it could be applied in policy analysis, organizational structures, or constitutional formation.

Analyses of Collective Action and Coordination Situations

The difference between collective action situations and coordination situations was clarified by making the preferences and alternative natural strategies of agents the basis of analysis. Preferences and strategies are the proper basis for a taxonomy of types of situations. Using this distinction, we saw how the spontaneous order tradition from Hume to Hayek confused two distinct types of situations.

Externality

Based on an analysis of the general concept externality, we saw that there are at least three distinguishable types: intentional, accidental, and incidental. The distinction makes possible a rigorous determination of the roles of normative constraints in relation to externalities.

Consider now some important implications of the results of our analysis.

Implications for Economic Theory

In addition to specifying the presuppositions of the First Fundamental Theorem of Welfare Economics, at least four fundamental concepts in economic theory can be refined: market, perfect competition, perfectly competitive market, and externality.

Market

The concept of a market is of critical importance to economic theory. However, there is no consensus or even widely accepted explication of the concept of a market.[1] Moss (1984) wrote, "For all that is written about the market and market forces, it is remarkably difficult to find a definition of 'the market' in the textbooks or other economic literature." The term *market* is used alternatively to denote either social behavior or a social situation composed of individuals, commodities, and other types of nonnormative conditions on trade. However, we have shown that a market is best characterized as an institutional framework for trade composed of conventions and moral normative constraints. This lack of consensus regarding the concept of a market carries over into the next concept, perfect competition.

Perfect Competition

Perfect competition is a type of social interaction. The First Fundamental Theorem of Welfare Economics states that "every competitive equilibrium allocation is Pareto optimal." It presupposes that every individual acts perfectly competitively. Perfect competition exists only when every individual acts as a price-taker, that is, only when every agent takes market actions only. Thus, perfect competition is trade in the absence of collusion, market power, externalities, and force or fraud of any kind.

Perfectly Competitive Market

Since the idea of individuals acting perfectly competitively is an essential concept, we should distinguish between perfect competition and a perfectly competitive market. A *perfectly competitive market* is a set of normative conditions that ensures perfect competition. Perfect competition exists only in and because of a perfectly competitive market. The standard textbook definition of a perfectly competitive market portrays it as a natural social situation constituted by numerous participants, no barriers to exit or entry, homogeneous products, and perfect information. However, Hurwicz (1972) shows that even under these conditions agents will have both an incentive to misrepresent their true demand and the means to defraud others to gain for oneself. Thus, the standard definition of a perfectly competitive market is not sufficient to ensure perfect competition. My analysis has shown that perfect competition requires a system of moral normative conditions. A perfectly competitive market must be treated as an institution that includes not only a set of coordinating norms but also a set of moral normative constraints which make perfect competition possible.

These considerations suggest that it would be helpful to maintain a distinction between various usages of the term *market*. Besides denoting an institutional framework for trade composed of two different kinds of rules, a market also denotes a social situation comprised by an institutional framework, individuals, and commodities. Call the first version an I-market and the second an S-market. Thus, we could say that perfect competition (as social behavior) requires the existence of a perfectly competitive I-market. We can also say that a perfectly competitive S-market (an actual market comprised of price-taking agents and commodities) requires that the conditions of perfect competition hold (i.e., it presupposes a perfectly competitive I-market).

Externality

As I mentioned in Chapter 5, many theorists complain that the concept of an externality is not well defined. There is a lack of specificity and of consensus among scholars in philosophy, economics, and legal theory regarding externality. Even as late as 1994, Andreas A. Papandreou (1994: 2) wrote,

Given the importance of externality in economic theory, and the effort put into characterizing externality, it is surprising how hazy a concept it has remained. Extending the empty box metaphor, not only has there not been consensus on what externality should signify, but the box seems to be semi-opaque, preventing a clear understanding of what the different ideas are. The present intuitive notion of externality as activities that take place outside market transactions, belies the difficulties that arise the minute one tries to give analytical content to this intuition, treating it as a separate category of market failure.

An *externality* is the effect of some action related to production or consumption that imposes an involuntary cost or benefit on some other agent and for which no compensation is made. We may distinguish between intentional, accidental, and incidental externalities. Externalities are usually understood as being the incidental effects of the acts of production and consumption. The effects of acts of theft and deceit are intentional externalities. For want of a better term, and to distinguish between incidental and intentional externalities, I have referred to the negative effects on the well-being of individuals resulting from acts done negligently, mistakenly, inadvertently, carelessly, involuntarily, or otherwise unintentionally[2] as accidental externalities. Each type must be either precluded or rectified to achieve efficient outcomes.

In Chapter 2, I presented a version of the First Fundamental Theorem of Welfare Economics given a set of standard assumptions under which efficient allocations of commodities are socially achieved. I then compared the assumptions of that version of the First Welfare Theorem with those of the social situation in which moral normative constraints are absent. We saw that a thorough understanding of any proof of the First Welfare Theorem must include the role of every relevant assumption. In Chapter 6, we saw that a system of moral normative constraints, conventions for equilibrating supply and demand, and conventions and moral normative constraints for internalizing externalities are the necessary background assumptions of the First Fundamental Theorem of Welfare economics.

In sum, a market is an institution and perfect competition is a type of social interaction secured by a set of normative conditions, which includes moral normative constraints and which "internalizes" externalities. A distinction should be maintained between intentional, incidental, and accidental externalities, which are the effects of actions not governed by normative conditions. It follows that a perfectly competitive market includes a set of moral normative constraints and that any proof of the First Welfare Theorem presupposes this general set of normative conditions.

Implications for Political Theory and Moral Philosophy

These results carry over to political theory and moral philosophy. In particular they logically entail that the Invisible Hand Claim is mistaken. Just what is the Invisible Hand Claim? Adam Smith (1776: 456) is commonly considered to have first expressed the claim. Smith wrote:

As every individual, therefore, endeavors as much as he can both to employ his capital in the support of domestic industry, and so to direct that industry that its produce may be of the greatest value; every individual necessarily labors to render the annual revenue of the society as great as he can. He generally, indeed neither intends to promote the public interest, nor knows how much he is promoting it. By preferring the support of domestic to that of foreign industry, he intends only his own security; and by directing that industry in such a manner as its produce may be of the greatest value, he intends only his own gain, and he is in this, as in many other cases, led by an *invisible hand* [italics added] to promote an end which was no part of his intention.

But as we saw in Chapter 1, we are not quite sure exactly what he meant. Other academic writers who refer to Smith are also not sufficiently specific. Some theorists seem to indicate that as long as a group of people simply pursue their own interests according to a set of price conventions only, everyone will be better off. This is the Invisible Hand Claim.

There is an implicit subtle irony in the claim, which arrests one's attention: Selfishness achieves common good; thus, morality is not required when it comes to market interaction. To evaluate this claim, we took the irony at face value and described pure selfishness. We discovered that purely selfish agents pursuing their own interests must also possess internal incentives to comply with a particular set of moral norms to achieve their "common good."

David Gauthier (1986) also makes the Invisible Hand Claim, claiming that a perfectly competitive market is a "morally-free zone." Gauthier (1986: 84) wrote that a perfectly competitive market, "Were it realized, would constitute a morally-free zone, a zone within which the constraints of morality would have no place." If, as Gauthier claimed, the constraints of morality have no place in a perfectly competitive market, then either the set of presuppositions of a perfectly competitive market contains some nonnormative mechanism sufficient in itself to preclude such types of actions, or else agents, for nonnormative reasons, simply refrain from the use of force or of fraud. In other words, by claiming that "the constraints of morality have no place," it looks as though Gauthier must also hold that the presuppositions he cited have no moral normative force, yet are somehow sufficient to prevent agents from taking actions that generate inefficient outcomes of trade (i.e., using force or giving false information).

Several arguments showing why such a view is mistaken deserve discussion. First, Gauthier intended to show that, in practice, morality arises from market failure and began his argument by stating what he considered to be the conditions of a perfectly competitive market: "Individual factor endowments and private goods, free market activity and mutual unconcern, and the absence of externalities – these are the presuppositions of a perfectly competitive market" (1986: 89). Since Gauthier claimed that the constraints of morality have no place in a perfectly competitive market, we might try to ascertain how a perfectly competitive market, as he described it, precludes actions such as theft and fraud. Of his five stated presuppositions, only "free market activity" or "the absence of externalities" might be able to secure perfect competition.[3] Externalities are either intentional, incidental, or accidental effects on the well-being of another for which no compensation is made. We showed in Chapter 3 that to presume that nonmarket actions are never taken by a group of purely selfish people leads to a contradiction. So the "absence of externalities" presupposition will not work.

On the other hand, Gauthier's position entails a second contradiction, depending on what he means by the term *free activity*. Gauthier asserted that "the presupposition of *free activity* ensures that no one is subject to any form of compulsion, or to any type of limitation not already affecting her actions as a solitary individual" (1986: 96). However, he did not explain how free activity actually works "to ensure that no one is subject to any form of compulsion" and he did not indicate what kinds of limitations (constraints) "already affect" agents' actions.

Gauthier refers to *free activity* as a presupposition, that is, as a basic notion not itself reducible to some combination of other assumptions. However, it is not at all clear that he treats it as a presupposition. He wrote, "Thus the market involves the entirely free activity of each individual, limited only by the factors and products that he owns, the production functions that determine the possibilities of transforming factors into products, and the utility functions of others that determine the possibilities of exchange" (1986: 86). Now, he could not define "ownership" in terms that involve moral normative constraints, for that would be to build moral normative constraints into the model in the first place. Perhaps he should have used the term *controls* instead of the term *owns*. Thus,

I may interpret him as simply observing that an agent's freedom is limited by budget constraints, production constraints, and the preferences of other people. Aside from these physical constraints, an agent can do whatever she pleases. Thus, these physical constraints do not define free activity; they demarcate the limits of free activity, that is, they define an agent's natural strategy domain.

Nothing in Gauthier's concept of free activity prevents an agent from stealing if he has the opportunity to do so. There is no mechanism to preclude theft and fraud. Gauthier indicated that someone has ownership of some factor if and only if he may "use it as he pleases in the processes of production, exchange, and consumption" (Gauthier 1986: 86). He even referred to this particular freedom as a "right to ownership" (Gauthier 1986: 86). But he could not assert that a right to ownership is a moral right for that would be to smuggle morality into the model in the first place.

Gauthier elaborated on his idea of free activity by indicating that "A person is free in so far as she is able, without interference, to direct her capacities to the service of her preferences" (1986: 90). And, "My argument is that in a perfectly competitive market, mutual advantage is assured by the *unconstrained* [emphasis added] activity of each individual in pursuit of her own greatest satisfaction, so that there is no place, rationally for constraint" (1986: 13) The free activity assumption in these quotes looks like a liberty right. But again he is careful not to define it in terms of a moral right because that would introduce morality – as he defines it – into the assumption set of the market. Thus, Gauthier is caught in a dilemma. He construed a perfectly competitive market as a morally free zone and specified free activity as one of its presuppositions. However, to portray the market as morally free, that is, as not requiring moral normative constraints, he could not specify free activity in terms of the effects of either a property right or a liberty right. On the other hand, for free activity to function as he described it, he must specify free activity resulting from either a property right or a liberty right, which functions (along with sufficient internal incentives to comply) as a moral normative constraint. Therefore, if Gauthier claimed both that free activity is a presupposition of perfectly competitive markets and that perfectly competitive markets do not require moral normative constraints, his account entails a contradiction.

Let us consider an alternative interpretation, which places his views in a stronger position. A distinction is sometimes made between the normative constraints *of* markets and those *within* markets. The idea is that some set of conventions and normative constraints constitutes the institutional framework of markets and that it is either irrelevant or irrational for any individual to observe any other moral constraint on her pursuit of self-interest. Perhaps Gauthier intended to be understood in this sense, that is, that markets are morally free from *additional* moral normative constraints, but not from the morally relevant constraints that constitute the institutional framework of markets. Gauthier (1982: 42) wrote,

Smith and the *laissez faire* economists of the late eighteenth and early nineteenth centuries had arrived at one of the most significant discoveries in the moral realm – the discovery of a framework of human interaction within which the interests of each would harmonize free from any form of constraint, so that individual gain and mutual benefit would necessarily converge. Justice would be of concern in establishing the framework, but of no concern within it. The framework is the perfectly competitive market.

Gauthier is not clear regarding his interpretation of Adam Smith and other early economists; that is, he is not clear on their ideas regarding the process of "establishing" a perfectly competitive market, and not explicit regarding how justice is "of concern." Suppose that Gauthier meant that universal observance of just rules is a necessary condition for efficient outcomes of trade. Furthermore, suppose that, by indicating that justice is "of no concern" within a perfectly competitive market, Gauthier meant that to subject one's economic decisions to moral constraints, besides those that form the institutional framework of markets, is either irrelevant or irrational. By using the term *justice,* Gauthier referred to Smith's proviso regarding the working of the invisible hand: "as long as he does not violate the laws of justice." For Smith, the "laws of justice" are moral presuppositions of positive law. Hence, the normative constraints *of* markets are moral. Therefore, individuals must morally constrain their behavior for the sake of efficiency. If this is so, then it is at least confusing, if not contradictory, for Gauthier to say that "morality has no application in conditions of perfect competition" (1982: 47). For that would be to claim both that morality is a necessary condition of perfect competition and that no more morality is necessary beyond the morality that is necessary. Either way, it is misleading at best to say that perfectly competitive markets are morally free. Moreover, before one can determine which moral constraints are superfluous, one must first determine which are necessary. Gauthier does not state which normative constraints are required for efficient outcomes of trade.

To interpret Gauthier so as to avoid the problems raised thus far, I could understand him as differing with Smith on the meaning of the "laws of justice" holding that the normative constraints *of* markets are legal constraints that render moral normative constraints *within* markets unnecessary. In this case, neither property rights nor liberty rights need be construed as moral constraints, but they could be seen as State-enforced claims – as legal constraints, not moral constraints. Therefore, even if free activity is secured by property rights and a liberty right, the market is indeed a morally free zone.

I need not delve further into the complex relationship between law and morality. It is enough simply to note that Gauthier (1982: 41) himself defined morality as a "constraint on the pursuit of self-interest." The constraints of morality differ from other kinds of constraints that agents face in market interaction (e.g., budget constraints). Moral constraints are normative, and the others are positive. It is not clear on what grounds the constraints *of* markets could be legal, but not moral. Intuitively, it is hard to construe a prohibition against stealing, for example, as being legal, but not moral. And note that this interpretation of Gauthier is purchased at the expense of a misinterpretation of Adam Smith's view of justice.

In his *Lectures on Jurisprudence* (1763: 7), Smith wrote, "The first and chief design of all civill [sic] governments, is, as I observed, to preserve justice amongst the members of the state and prevent all incroachments [sic] on the individualls [sic] in it, from others of the same society. – {That is, to maintain each individual in his perfect rights.}" Smith divided the set of "perfect rights" into two subsets – natural rights and acquired rights. *Natural rights* are rights persons hold by virtue of being persons. Natural rights are prelegal rights, that is, moral rights. *Acquired rights* are rights held by virtue of citizenship. Nevertheless, even acquired rights have their basis in morality. Smith (1763: 401) referred to his *A Theory of Moral Sentiments* in his account of the origin of the state to its ground in moral psychology. Therefore, it is a mistake to assert that Smith held a view of legal constraints as nonmoral.

Suppose we grant, for the sake of argument, that property rights and a liberty right are legal rights, but not moral rights. We showed in Chapter 4 that if individuals are not affected in any way by moral considerations, they will not behave competitively. The existence of legal constraints alone is not sufficient to constrain the behavior of strict rational egoists. Strict rational egoists will have both an incentive and the means to violate existing rights. Thus, the existence of legal constraints alone presents a collective action problem. Only if agents have an internal incentive to recognize and to observe others' rights will they behave competitively. In Chapter 4, we showed that, absent the State, the only solutions that solve collective action problems and involve internally based motives to comply are the moral principle solution and the dual utility solution. Both of these solutions involve morality in some respect. Therefore, a perfectly competitive market is not a morally free zone.

Finally, we showed in Chapter 6 that a right to autonomy is a necessary condition of competitive behavior. Since a right to autonomy is a moral right, a perfectly competitive market is not a morally free zone. Therefore, David Gauthier's claim regarding the relationship between morality and perfect competition is false.

Implications for Legal Theory

Appeals court judges and policy analysts often cite economic efficiency as a factor in their decisions and proposals. Since economic efficiency requires moral normative constraints, appellate decisions and policy recommendations based on standards of economic efficiency must not ignore the moral rights that are the necessary conditions of economic efficiency. Otherwise, there is the risk of defeating the effects of those moral normative constraints. When such constraints are thereby undercut, efficiency cannot be achieved, and it proves futile to use economic efficiency as a standard for legal decision making.

There is a further implication for legal theory that deserves review. The moral conditions of economic efficiency set moral and logical limits on the kinds of things that can be commodified. The setting of those limits ultimately depends on the goal of economic efficiency. We therefore have a moral grounding for laws preventing some types of things from becoming commodities. Anyone who also desires to achieve economically efficient outcomes of trade must agree. Thus, even though the right is moral, debate over its application is avoided on the grounds of a consensus regarding economic efficiency as a goal to be achieved and sustained.

In Chapter 5, I argued that every policy prescription can be seen as an attempt to realize some assumption of the First Welfare Theorem. Given the "incomplete or absence of markets" concept of an externality, it follows that procedures used to correct market failure are, in effect, procedures for expanding the commodity space, that is, for letting more kinds of things become commodities.

Judge Richard Posner's property rights assignment principle is an example of a procedure that "internalizes" externalities by expanding the commodity space. Recall from Chapter 5 that his assignment principle is this: Given the assumption that common law can be explained as the attempt to maximize wealth and that exclusive and transferable property rights are sufficient for the efficient use of resources were it not for transaction costs, in property rights disputes where the law is either unclear or undeveloped, courts should simply mimic market outcomes by assigning entitlements to those who would have valued them most where voluntary exchange is feasible. Adverse effects on others caused by an agent producing or consuming are externalities and are internalized when the right to the property in question is assigned to whomever values it the most. Nevertheless, if the moral rights that are the necessary conditions of economic efficiency are ignored, there are no grounds based on economic efficiency by which to limit the kinds of things that can be commodified.

In a famous paper on property law, Calabresi and Melamed (1972) suggested that inalienability rules, which are grounded in moral considerations, may limit the procedures for internalizing externalities. But Posner suggested that there are no limits except administrative costs. The "incomplete markets" view of externalities implies that any aspect of any state of affairs that is also the object of some agent's desire is a tradable commodity. A logical limit would exist if some desire cannot be converted into commodities without undercutting the very conditions that make Pareto-optimal allocations of commodities possible. For example, commodifying persons and enslaving them against their wishes denies their rights to autonomy. Even though a slave's preferences continue to range over alternative social states, she is unable to take those actions that she thinks will maximize utility. Hence, allocations of commodities cannot be Pareto optimal. Thus, based on the goal of economic efficiency human beings cannot themselves become commodities. Unless, of course, a society may choose not to count the preferences of slaves. This is historically true, but it does not apply to early twenty-first century democratic societies.[4]

Summary and Concluding Comments

In Chapter 2, a framework for analyzing social situations that enables us to answer rigorously our two central questions was developed. The framework is composed of two divisions corresponding to the two essential aspects of social situations. The first division regards agents; the second, the situation in which they interact. Agents are depicted in terms of their preferences and their rationality. The situation within which agents act is defined in terms of positive and normative conditions.

Using this framework, a particular type of social situation was modeled in which agents, who are purely selfish and fully rational, interact in the absence of moral normative constraints; that is, they interact under pure anarchy. I call this particular type of social situation Strict Rational Egoism.

We saw that the presuppositions of the First Fundamental Theorem of Welfare Economics (or the First Welfare Theorem) are not the assumptions of Strict Rational Egoism. The incompatibility between what the First Welfare Theorem assumes and what Strict Rational Egoism allows points to the ambiguity regarding the role of moral normative constraints in the First Welfare Theorem and underscores the need to examine the role of moral normative constraints. If the First Welfare Theorem implicitly assumes a set of moral normative constraints, then it is not a proof of the common understanding of Adam Smith's claim regarding the invisible hand.

In Chapter 3, we saw that a population of strict rational egoists cannot achieve efficient allocations of commodities through market interaction in the absence of moral normative constraints because moral normative constraints are necessary conditions of competitive behavior. There are three reasons why moral normative constraints are necessary conditions of competitive behavior. First, a presumption against nonmarket action entails a contradiction. Second, under a widely accepted conception of a "perfectly competitive market," individuals have both an incentive and the means to violate the rules of the process. Third, even if we alter assumptions (p_5) and (p_6) so that agents have maximal information-processing capabilities and perfect information regarding every economically relevant variable, there exists a possibility in which no agent will be able to make a decision.

A Spontaneous Order Objection might be raised against the conclusion of Chapter 3, claiming that the social behavior of selfish individuals in a situation depicted by the specified assumptions of the framework will converge into regular patterns and that, in turn, will be sufficient to produce optimal outcomes of trade.

In Chapter 4, this objection was refuted. First, a rigorous distinction is made between coordination situations and collective action situations and the role of convention is further developed. We see that conventions are not normative constraints. Furthermore, only moral normative constraints – partially constituted by collective action rules – can coordinate agents' strategies in Collective Action Situations. An exchange situation is a collective action situation. After discussing five types of possible solutions to collective action situations we saw that the Spontaneous Order Objection holds only if there is a solution to an exchange situation that arises out of Strict Rational Egoism. But there is no such solution.

In short, strict rational egoists will not comply with rules because exchange situations are collective action situations and of the five possible types of solutions to collective action situations, none will be adopted be strict rational egoists. Therefore, the Spontaneous Order Objection fails.

In Chapter 5, it was demonstrated that a population of strict rational egoists cannot achieve efficient allocations of commodities through trade by showing that in the absence of moral normative constraints no means exist for internalizing externalities. There are three distinct types of externalities – intentional, accidental, and incidental externalities. It is demonstrated that economic efficiency is not possible for strict rational egoists because, without moral normative constraints, externalities cannot be precluded or rectified.

In Chapter 6, it was demonstrated that the normative presuppositions of market interaction leading to efficient outcomes include a system of moral normative constraints, a set of conventions for equilibrating supply and demand, and a set of moral normative constraints and conventions for internalizing intentional, accidental, and incidental externalities. The system of moral normative constraints is specified as a normative social practice in which

(i)   A set of moral rights – construed as a set of moral Hohfeldian positions that restrict agents' natural and rational strategy domains – provides a moral basis for internalizing externalities,
(ii) Each agent has some sufficient internal incentive to comply with these rights, and
(iii) There exists a set of procedures according to which agents hold each other responsible.

Together, the system of moral normative constraints and the conventions constitute one set of background presuppositions of the First Fundamental Theorem of Welfare Economics.

Pareto-optimal equilibrium allocations of commodities cannot be achieved through trade without agents' actions being morally constrained. In short, there are moral conditions of economic efficiency. Thus, while we may speak metaphorically of an Invisible Hand guiding social behavior, we must bear in mind that its guidance is moral. Furthermore, any theoretical or practical endeavor that depends on a concept of economic efficiency must take the moral conditions of efficiency into consideration.

Notes

1. Introduction and Synopsis

1 An *outcome of market interaction* is a distribution of commodities among traders; and an *efficient outcome* is one to which there is no other possible alternative outcome in which at least one person is better off and no one worse off. In this work *efficiency* is meant to be understood as Pareto optimality. Pareto optimality is a standard for comparing well-being among alternative social states. An allocation of commodities (or a social state defined in terms of each agent's consumption bundle) is Pareto optimal if and only if there is no possible alternative social state that is Pareto superior to it. A social state σ_1 is *Pareto superior* to σ_2 if and only if at least one person is better off (measured in terms of more of at least one commodity) under σ_1 than under σ_2 and no one is worse off. I will develop this in more detail in the next chapter. We should bear in mind that we will not consider the goal of economically efficient allocations of commodities to include the "internalization" of beneficial externalities.

2 Amartya Sen (1977:341) observes that "Admitting behavior based on commitment [read: "moral commitment"] would, of course have far reaching consequences on the nature of economic models."

3 Smith used the phrase, "invisible hand," only three times: once in *An Inquiry Into the Nature and Causes of the Wealth of Nations* (1776), once in *A Theory of Moral Sentiments* (1759), and once in the *Essays on Philosophical Subjects* (1795).

4 See Evensky (1993: 197–205) and Trebilcock (1993: 259, 267).

5 Indeed, Cooter and Ulen (1997: 7) claim that "economics does not have a detailed account of what it means for exchange to be voluntary."

6 This account is compatible with the accounts given by David Copp (1995) and D. W. Haslett (1994).

7 It would be redundant if it were analyzed as an obligation to fulfill one's obligations. If one has obligations, it is not necessary to add an obligation to fulfill obligations.

8 I am following a distinction specified in Ostrom, Gardner, and Walker (1994: 26): "we ... distinguish between the types of constraints that affect the structure of a game: the constraints of the physical and biological world and the constraints imposed by the rules that individuals evolve or design to limit what can be done in a particular set-

ting." Although these and other theorists do not use the terms, *positive constraint* and *normative constraint,* what they refer to by their terms is similar, if not identical, to the referents of the terms I use. See also North (1990: 384,6), Frey (1992: 10), Buchanan (1989: 41–6), and Myerson (1989: 191). Second, a distinction is sometimes made between constitutive rules and regulative rules. In this book, we will encounter both types and will treat them both as elements of normative constraints. See Heap and Varoufakis (1995: 30–1).

9 I modify the framework of analysis of social situations developed by Ostrom et al. (1994).

10 See the empirical study on the motivations of those who rescued Jews during the Holocaust in Oliner and Oliner (1988).

11 Traditional understandings of externalities consider what can be termed incidental and accidental externalities. I add intentional externalities to complete the taxonomy of broad types of costs or benefits not captured by market interaction. These three types can be related to tort law, property law, and the criminal law.

12 The theorem always presupposes that externalities are absent and that agents behave competitively. But various proofs of the theorem may cite alternative additional assumptions. For example, proofs of the theorem may presuppose that agents' preference relations are monotonic or locally nonsatiated (monotonic preference relations imply locally nonsatiated preference relations). Some accounts of the theorem build some crucial assumptions into the statement itself. In Mas-Colell, Whinston, and Green (1995: 326), for example, the theorem is formally stated as follows:

If the price p^* and allocation $(x_1^*, \ldots, x_I^*, q_1^*, \ldots, x_J^*)$ constitute a competitive equilibrium, then this allocation is Pareto optimal.

A competitive equilibrium, in this version, is an allocation of goods and a set of prices p^* for those goods if (1) each firm chooses a production plan that maximizes profits taking p^* as given for his inputs and output, (2) each consumer chooses a consumption bundle that maximizes utility given his budget constraint given p^*, and (3) all markets clear.

2. A Contextualized Proof of the First Fundamental Theorem of Welfare Economics

1 I am indebted to Elinor Ostrom et al. (1994), to James Coleman (1990), and to Joseph Greenberg (1990).

2 Ostrom et al. (1994: 25) refer to the framework they developed as the Institutional Analysis and Development (IAD) framework. Its basic conceptual unit is an *action arena* consisting of two parts: the Action Situation and Actors. An *action situation* "is characterized using seven clusters of variables: (1) participants, (2) positions, (3) actions, (4) potential outcomes, (5) a function that maps actions into realized outcomes, (6) information, (7) the costs and benefits assigned to actions and outcomes (1994: 29)." *Actors* are characterized by four variables: (1) their preferences, (2) their information processing capabilities, (3) the selection criteria they follow in making decisions (e.g., the minimax criterion), and (4) the resources at their disposal.

3 Cp. Sen (1980).

4 The idea of agents choosing from among alternative social states is explained further when I discuss assumption (p_3).

5 Each agent's preferences range over alternative social states defined solely in terms of his or her own consumption bundles.

6 To exclude morally relevant effects on actions effectively, we must be cognizant of the problems of modeling morally relevant factors. A common approach is to differentiate *internal* from *external* influences on agents' behavior. Vanberg (1994: 44), citing an example of an internal influence, treated morality as a "dispositional variable . . . [which] reflects a person's general disposition or propensity to act in accordance with moral principles, relatively independently of the specific incentive structure inherent in particular choice settings." In discussing the problems of how to introduce morality into economic models Vanberg (1994: 44) wrote,

> Attempts to account for a dispositional variable, like morality, in economic explanations seem to be at odds with the standard economic classification of explanatory variables into either *preferences* or *constraints*. As normally understood, this classification corresponds to the 'subjective vs objective' distinction: preferences being the subjective, intrapersonal determinants of choice, and constraints being the objective, external determinants. Given this system of reference, introducing a variable, morality, into economic explanations would seem to require us either to classify morality as a subjective, intrapersonal preference-variable or as an objective, external constraint variable.

For the purposes of this chapter, we need not review Vanberg's conception of morality or the way he proposes to model it. I simply want to call attention to the distinction Vanberg mentions and to the recognized problem of modeling morally relevant influences either as preferences or as constraints.

7 Note that James Coleman (1990), Loren E. Lomasky (1987), and Alan Gewirth (1978) all suggested that there is a logical connection between purposive action and rights. I do not discuss philosophical grounds of rights. I am only interested in the role of rights in the achievement of efficient allocations of commodities. My argument might have some bearing on these theorists' claims, but exploring such connections is beyond the scope of this analysis.

8 See Becker (1976: 5).

9 I take this definition from Mas-Colell et al. (1995: 6). In a footnote, the authors mentioned two issues of importance to us. First, there is no agreement within the field regarding terminology. Some accounts use *weakly ordered* or *complete preorder* instead of *rational*. Second, some presentations include the *reflexive condition*. But since reflexivity is implied by completeness, we leave it out. Furthermore, this understanding of rational preferences is open to challenge on empirical grounds. It is possible that, on an alternative understanding of *rational*, some individual may prefer one thing over a second, the second over the third, and the third over the first. I am not developing an empirical model. I am determining, with mathematical rigor, what purely selfish agents can achieve. So I adopt the understanding of rational preferences, which is standard in advanced economic theory.

10 In Chapter 6, I introduce into the model moral normative constraints which involves changes in both the agent set and situation set. Then the derived principle for action is for agents who possess sufficient internal incentives to comply with the rules. In this case, the derived principle for action must be modified to account for these changes.

DPA*: For any person i, action a_n^i, and state of affairs σ_n,
  i will take a_n^i if and only if
    (1) (i) i prefers σ_n, and
         (ii) i has good reason to believe that a_n^i is the best feasible means
             to achieve σ_n, and
         (iii) there are no rules that prohibit actions of type a_n^i, or
    (2) (i)   there are rules that require a_n^i.

11 Compare Baumol and Blinder (1991: 174).

12 Money is a public good whose creation involves norms other than those of practical rationality (Arrow 1969: 34).

13 Note the relationship: Roles are filled by a class of individuals that may or may not be coextensive with the set of all individuals. Rules are relative to roles.

14 See also *protocol statements* in Hirshleifer (1985).

15 As I will explain in detail later, conventions coordinate the actions of several agents but do not constrain any.

16 Macleod (1996) discussed a variety of standards with a view to clarifying Adam Smith's notion of the common good.

17 The auctioneer is an element in Leon Walras' (1874) seminal analysis of competitive general equilibrium.

18 Alternatively, a consumption bundle of agent i is denoted by $C_v^i = \mathbb{R}_+^m$.

19 This assumes that (1) $C^i = \mathbb{R}_+^m$, $i = 1, \ldots, n$, where C^i denotes the set of all bundles individually feasible for consumer i, (2) there is no free disposal, and (3) we are dealing with a pure exchange economy.

20 *Price-taking* indicates a type of market behavior defined partially by an agent's belief that he cannot affect the price by any other action. He makes his trading decisions entirely based on announced prices.

21 This proof follows the pattern of Proposition (16.C.1) in Mas-Collell et al. (1995, p. 549). A slightly stronger version of this theorem was originally proved by T. C. Koopmans (1957, First Essay, Proposition 4, p. 49).

22 By relations (16.C.1) and (16.C.2) in Mas-Colell et al. (1995, p. 549), (3.1) implies $p^*y > p^*w^{i\cdot}$ and (3.2) implies $p^*y^r \geq p^*w^r$.

3. The Moral Thesis

1 (p_5) Agents are sufficiently and instrumentally rational. (p_6) Agents are constrained by a perfectly competitive market: numerous participants, homogeneous products, freedom of exit and entry, and perfect information.

2 That is, agents are constrained by a perfectly competitive market: numerous participants, homogeneous products, freedom of exit and entry, and perfect information.

3 Individuals in the environment we describe are strict rational egoists, and we stipulate the absence of moral normative constraints. Hurwicz's economic environments are those situations in which individuals are price-takers, preferences are locally nonsatiated, commodities are perfectly divisible, and monopolies, externalities, and increasing returns to scale are absent.

4 Formally defined, a game-form $G = (N, S, h)$ for a set N of n players is defined by a

set S^i of admissible strategies for each $i \in N$, and by the outcome function, $h: S \rightarrow Z$, where S is the Cartesian product of the S^is, and Z is the outcome space.

5 (p_6) Agents are constrained by a perfectly competitive market: numerous participants, homogeneous products, freedom of exit and entry, and perfect information.

6 Actually, the proviso that the decision be made simultaneously rather than sequentially applies only when an agent is given no opportunity to change his mind after he understands what others will do. When agents make decisions sequentially and each has at least one opportunity to change his decision once he knows what every one else is doing, the proviso is unnecessary.

7 This assumption clearly shows the essential role of moral normative constraints and the detrimental consequences of not rigorously specifying and modeling them in the First Welfare Theorem.

8 Our account follows Ostrom et al. (1994: 34). It is also compatible with the concept of a "social situation" in Greenberg (1990).

9 An easily accessible explication of the concept of a Universal Turing Machine is given in Beckman (1980: 183–4). Alternative proofs are given in Davis (1973: 64), Malitz (1979: 95–9), and Yasuhara (1971: 28–30).

10 This is Alan Turing's (1936) thesis. See also Boolos and Jeffrey (1989: 20, 54).

11 In this book, I will not prove that each function is effectively computable and that each set or relation is effectively enumerable. Nevertheless, perhaps this much is worth noting: Proving that a function is effectively computable or that a set or relation is effectively enumerable using Universal Turing Machine descriptions is cumbersome. Since the class of partial recursive functions is coextensive with the class of partial Turing-computable functions, it would be less cumbersome to show that, for any function f, individuals in my model can (cannot) compute f, if f is (is not) partially recursive.

12 Each agent knows (1) every relevant characteristic regarding every agent including, of course, himself, (2) the value of every relevant variable in the situation, (3) that every other individual knows (1) and (2); and (4) that everyone knows (3).

13 Technically speaking, the domain of the function $f_i : \mathbb{N} \rightarrow \mathbb{N}$ is a finite subset of names of positive integers. Hence, for each individual in $I = \{1, \ldots, n\} \subseteq \mathbb{N}$, the function associates a name of a positive integer with a name of an individual; no two individuals have the same name. But we will ignore this technicality.

14 The conditions to which we refer can be conceived of as type-variables so that individuals are not required to know every conceivable configuration of conditions, but only the features of conditions that affect her choice of a strategy. Sets of actual conditions are members of classes (types) of conditions differentiated by their respective relevant defining features.

15 See Varian (1992: 95–7).

16 Notice that, by itself, the absence of common knowledge does not render the actions of other individuals irrelevant.

17 Also, we can suppose each agent is "programmed" to recognize potentially infinite loops. This supposition is not subject to the results of the Halting Problem for Turing Machines. The Halting Problem shows that there is a function that is not Turing computable. A function h is defined so that, given any of a set of Turing Machine programs associated with a set of functions only some of which are computable, it would determine whether or not the program will halt. There is no Turing Machine

that can compute the function h. The inputs of a decision function, on the other hand, are each effectively computable; thus, each are Turing computable. When computing a set of inputs such as the values of the utility functions associated with Table 3, a Turing Machine will either halt in some nonstandard position and fail to give an output, or it will enter a loop from which there is no exit. A Turing Machine can be programmed to identify potentially infinite loops in decision functions because decisions functions involve recursion from a double basis. Either way, we may suppose that the computational process ends.

18 In the first argument given in Chapter 2, the perfect information component of assumption (p_6) did not extend to every individual's preference relation and natural strategy domain. In this argument, that is, in social situations defined by assumptions (p_1)–(p_9), agents have maximal information-processing capabilities, perfect information regarding every economically relevant variable in a context that requires simultaneous rather than sequential decisions in conjunction with the other conditions cited in assumption (p_6).

19 This is an important issue. There exists a debate between two broad types of conceptualizations of rights: a social choice conceptualization and a game-form conceptualization. Within each type there are variations, as one might expect. Regardless, for our purposes, we note the vital significance of the difference between a conceptualization that conceives of rights effectivity as functions over social states and one that depicts rights as restrictions on an agents' strategy profiles. We will adopt the second type of conception. See van Hees (1995), Sen (1992), Gaertner et al. (1992), and Sugden (1994).

20 It makes no difference that, in effect, individuals had no other option because the very purpose of enforced rights is to restrict the range of options.

4. A Spontaneous Order Objection

1 Even if it could be shown that a market, construed as a set of moral normative constraints and serving as a solution to a collective action situation, could emerge spontaneously when agents are construed differently than they are in the assumption set (i.e., as agents having moral motivations and not as strict rational egoists), it would be entirely compatible with our aims, for it would involve the concession that moral normative constraints are necessary.

2 For an alternative account of collective action situation, see Binmore (1994) who critiques the standard interpretation of PD situations. See also Greenberg (1990). Taylor (1990: 223) claimed that "all situations representable as Prisoners' Dilemma are collective action problems."

3 Edna Ullmann-Margalit (1977: *vii*) offers a taxonomy that includes only the first three types of situations. She confesses not to have any arguments for the exhaustiveness of the list. However, she believes that the first three are paradigmatic, and that any other types could be subsumed under one of them. Schotter (1981: 22) adds without argument the fourth type to Ullmann-Margalit's original three.

4 It can also lead to strictly Pareto-inferior results. See Taylor (1990: 223).

5 See also Greenberg (1990: 4) for similar observations regarding the limitations of game-theoretic accounts of social situations.

6 By using this list, we follow the analysis of Coval and Smith (1986: 2). What we in-

troduce here is important for our concept of morality as a social practice as it makes provision to relieve liability. It is not necessary at this point to give more detail.

7 If the situation is noncooperative, that is, since agents are not able to negotiate agreements, it is a matter of coordinating strategies accidentally.

8 I add this caveat regarding normative constraints and the "possibility" of strategies conflicting because later on I want to discuss in detail how normative constraints convert collective action situations into coordination situations. It is in this sense that Adam Smith's Invisible Hand "coordinates" the activities of numerous individuals. I conclude that this is the role of Smith's "laws of justice."

9 Lewis (1969) showed how such a rule could emerge among a population of rational egoists.

10 What follows is adapted from Nida-Rümelin (1991).

11 See Margolis (1982, 1984, 1990).

12 See Axelrod (1984).

13 This solution differs from (2) in that such moral principles are understood to be held in common.

14 Compare to Michael Taylor (1990: 224) in which the author defines an *internal solution* to a collective action situation as one that does not require a change either in agents' existing preferences and beliefs or in the rule-structure of the situation.

15 See Axelrod (1984) and Hardin (1982).

16 In the terms suggested by Ostrom et al. (1994), we iterate "play" only by replacing the "Default Payoff Condition," which indicates that "Any player can retain any outcome that the player can physically obtain and defend" with a rule that forbids that action under any conditions.

5. The Roles of Moral Normative Constraints in Relation to Externalities

1 Of course, there are other taxonomies: production and consumption externalities, positive and negative externalities, and technical and pecuniary externalities. These are compatible with the three-part taxonomy I am using. The three-part taxonomy emerges from a distinction between types of actions that cause externalities, not from a distinction between the consequences of actions.

2 Thus, to rule out externalities by assumption renders the First Welfare Theorem nearly tautologous.

3 However, even if such behaviors were fully commodified, that does not mean that the behaviors would cease. The existence of the behaviors depends only on their market value. If drug-taking, for instance, is valued more than it is disdained, then it will not cease. Drug-takers will only have to pay for their use. Of course, there may be connections such as increased health care premiums. Risk-averse people underwrite the protection of risk-takers.

4 Here is an example of an favorable externality. Landowner Alice keeps her mile of road frontage clear of debris and noxious weeds. Landowner Betty's house is across the road Alice's property. Betty values clean and neat roadsides. Thus, Betty gains a benefit from Alice for which no compensation is made.

5 See Posner (1992).

6 See Richard Posner, *The Economic Analysis of Law* (1992) and Cooter and Ulen (1997).

7 Agents are rational egoists instead of strict rational egoists.

8 *Kaldor-Hicks efficiency* is defined as follows: For any two states of affairs *A* and *B*, *A* is Kaldor-Hicks efficient compared to *B* iff at least one person *S* is sufficiently better off under *A* than under *B* so that *S* could compensate those who are worse off under *A* and still be better off.

9 Recall that we have stipulated that we are not dealing with positive externalities.

6. The Moral Conditions of Economic Efficiency

1 The concepts of exchange and of transaction have been subjected to extensive analysis by economists and social theorists. See James Coleman (1990) and John Davis (1992). We need not delve extensively into these discussions. Instead, consider the following definition for the sake constructing a picture of trade as social behavior. An *exchange* (or *transaction*) is an event analyzable in terms of at least two separate, but essentially connected, actions performed by two separate agents. Each act is defined as giving something (tangible or not) in return for something else. We grant that trade also presupposes production. Therefore efficient outcomes of trade also presuppose that producers maximize production functions.

2 See Lewis (1969); "convention"; Ullmann-Margalit (1977), "norm"; Schotter (1981), "social institution"; Petit (1990), "social norm"; Postema (1982), "law"; Reynolds (1989), "law." Let me briefly cite some examples. H. L. A. Hart (1994: *v*) treated morality as a social phenomenon and declares that, in addition to being an exercise in conceptual analysis, "[his] book may be regarded as an essay in descriptive sociology." David Lewis (1969: 3) referred to his work as "an analysis of our common, established concept of convention" but did so against a background of actual norms and imagined conditions of their emergence. Joseph Raz (1990: 15) analyzed norms "by explaining their relation to reasons for action." Edna Ullmann-Margalit (1977: 2) offered an analysis of three types of norms based on a rational reconstruction of the situations from which they could have emerged. She said that her methodology is explicative and explanatory, philosophical, but not empirical. Developing further the methodological concepts used by Lewis and Ullmann-Margalit, Andrew Schotter (1981: 21) offered accounts of social institutions by showing how they evolve from an "institutional state-of-nature." In offering her own analysis of social convention, Margaret Gilbert (1989: 20) found the accounts given by Lewis and by Hart to be "inadequate as accounts of the intuitive concept of a social convention." Finally, John Searle (1995) developed an account of social institutions based on an account of the conditions under which they are constructed. Searle's analysis depends on his theories of speech acts, of collective intentionality, and of rule-governed behavior.

3 See Bourdieu (1990) and Gilbert (1989: 20). There seem to be many kinds of sets of beliefs and practices (e.g., science, home building, gardening, etc.). Empirical morality is just one particular *kind* of set of beliefs and practices. Adherence to a particular empirical morality defines a particular group of people. The differences that seem to possess the greatest overriding force among human beings are not differences in race, gender, age, or ability, but differences in worldviews.

4 An empirical morality need not be consistent. That is, an empirical morality may entail beliefs or results that may conflict. However, these will be the exception rather than the rule and may not be readily apparent.

5 Even though a group's using the same language is a social practice simpliciter, it can be highly valued and can have important connections to individuals' identities.

6 See Marion Smiley (1992) on responsibility being attached not only to the individual but also to the community.

7 Forgiveness may not be a strategy for relieving liability as much as a strategy for readmission into full communal participation and good will. After an individual has repaired whatever damage that has been done, made restitution, paid compensation, etc., then it seems appropriate to forgive. Regardless, it is beyond the scope of this book to pursue these issues further. See Jean Hampton (1988).

8 See James Coleman (1990) on social capital.

9 Most of what I propose regarding the notion of a normative social practice and the idea of a responsibility schema I have learned from Ronald Koshoshek, although I have revised some of his ideas in ways he might not approve.

10 See Hurwicz (1996).

11 See van Hees (1995).

12 van Hees (1995) is a perfect example.

13 See Oliner and Oliner (1988).

14 See, for example, Steiner (1994) and Wellman (1982, 1985, 1995: 7–9), Becker (1977), Martin (1993), Munzer (1990: 17–22), and Thomson (1990).

15

Table N1. *Hohfeld's Fundamental Legal Conceptions*

Elements	Correlatives	Opposites
claim (right)	Duty	No right
Privilege (Liberty)	No right	Duty
Power	Liability	Disability (No power)
Immunity	Disability	Liability

Notice that in Table N1 Hohfeld's analysis involves three categories: elements, correlatives, and opposites. There are four basic elements: claims (or rights), privileges (or liberties), powers, and immunities. Hohfeld observes that the term *right* is used alternatively to denote either a claim, a privilege, a power, or an immunity, but it should be restricted to the notion of a claim to avoid needless confusion. However, following Hart (1994) and Wellman (1995), we may define claims, privileges, powers, and immunities as a set of Hohfeldian positions.

16 There are four classes of philosophical theories of rights: the claim theory, the interest (benefit) theory, the will (choice) theory, and the practice theory. Of the claim theory, Coleman and Kraus (1988: 35) wrote that "Rights entail legitimate claims." Joel Feinberg (1970: 90) expressed the theory slightly differently: "Having rights, of course, makes claiming possible; but it is claiming that gives rights their special moral importance." Under the interest theory, a right protects an interest. According to Hillel Steiner (1994: 58), a right exists if and only if "imposing or relaxing a constraint on some person's conduct . . . must be in conformity with what would generally better serve that other's important interests." According to the will (choice) theory, a right protects a choice. Steiner (1994: 58) claimed that a right exists if and only if "imposing or relaxing the constraint on some person's conduct, is another person's

choice to that effect." Finally, Rex Martin's (1993: 2) practice theory depicted rights as "institutional practices which require an institutional setting," or as "established patterns of acting or of being treated and hence [are] institutional in character."

We will not review existing criticisms of each of these classes of rights. Such a review involves much more than is pertinent to my presentation.

17 See Steiner (1994: 59, n9; 61n) and Wellman (1995: 7).

18 Lawrence Becker (1980) does this in presenting a "moral basis for property rights."

19 See Copp (1995), Schmidtz (1995), and Wellman (1995).

20 Nevertheless, Joel Feinberg (1970: 87) suggested a basis from which to distinguish moral rights from legal rights and in so doing provided a virtually uncontroversial rule of recognition for morality. He contended that legal rights differ from moral rights on the basis of validating claims:

> A man has a legal right when the official recognition of his claim (as valid) is called for by the governing rules. . . . A man has a moral right when he has a claim the recognition is called for – not (necessarily) by legal rules – but by moral principles, or the principles of an enlightened conscience.

21 Haslett (1994)

22 See James Coleman (1990); Gewirth (1978, 1993), Lomasky (1987), Rawls (1971), Raz (1990), and Tara Smith (1995).

23 Owen Flanagan (1991) reviewed objections to such a view.

24 In the absence of the State, a group of individuals will achieve efficient trade only by instituting a normative social practice. A normative social practice itself is constituted by at least one right. Such a right enables the social practice to function. However, such enabling or constitutive rights are not substantive in the sense that they preclude actions that directly undermine efficient trade. For example, giving false information that is directly pertinent to potential exchange is a type of action that directly precludes the achievement of Pareto-optimal allocations of commodities.

25 See Hampton (1997).

26 Hurwicz (1993) noted that "even where no third party is brought in, members of society may *play the role of intervenor* [emphasis added] vis-à-vis one another."

27 Of course, honesty could be construed as behavior that recognizes a moral principle that people ought to tell the truth. If the recognition of the moral principle also gives individuals a reason to act on the principle, then individuals will also have an incentive, thereby creating a moral normative constraint. However, such a construal of honesty is stronger than the view advocated here. Second, we will discuss in detail a right to true information as an aspect of a moral normative constraint necessary for efficient outcomes of trade in a later section. However, a right to true information as a condition for market efficiency is not unconditional. For practical and moral reasons, a right to true information cannot be a general right. Otherwise, everyone would have a claim against everyone else to provide true information about anything. Besides being impracticable, it conflicts with a right to privacy included in any empirical morality designed to achieve efficient outcomes of trade.

28 If individuals prefer a type of society (characterized by the absence of theft and fraud), then they must also prefer a type of character (similarly characterized) and, in turn, prefer the requisite decision rules. They must also prefer the procedural rules of a normative social practice. This permits us to incorporate the morality solution.

29 Samuel and Pearl Oliner (1988) discussed a study concerning what led people to risk their lives to help Jewish people during World War II. Rescuers grew up in homes having close family relationships. The value of attachment to others characterized parents' basic attitude toward all people, not only those in the immediate family. "Others rather than self were the primary focus for rescuers. Rescuers brought to the war a greater receptivity to others' needs." (161,2). Duties and rights were seen as the means to maintain attachment to others and to protect "the fabric that gives their lives order and meaning" (127).

30 Munzer (1990) and L. Becker (1977) synthesized the two analyses.

31 Later in his career, Honoré dropped one of the liability conditions of his analysis of ownership. Since I am referring to Becker's account of Honoré's analysis and since the details of this account of ownership are not essential to my argument (I argue only that some well-defined set of property rights are required and that this is an example of one such set), we will not need the full analysis for later discussion. I leave them as listed.

32 Wellman (1982) reviewed extant concepts of a right to welfare, each of which is stronger than the one proposed here. However, other theorists have denied that there is a right to welfare, basing their denial on the grounds of individuals' right to liberty, which in turn is grounded in some view of the person. For example, Tara Smith (1995: 206) wrote that "The alleged right to welfare, however, cannot be accepted since such a right could be respected only at the expense of individuals' freedom." It is beyond the scope of this book to review arguments for and against a right to welfare. I am simply attempting to state the necessary conditions of efficient trade. Nevertheless, a brief review of the structure of Smith's argument reveals a crucial asset held by my conception of a right to welfare.

Smith (1995: 18,7) indicated that "Rights are individuals' moral claims to freedom of action" and that "Freedom is essential for a person to engage in reasoned action, which in turn, is essential for the production of life sustaining goods and well-being." Smith rejected a right to welfare because it restricts freedom to act. She rightly assumed that individuals can live only if they consume life-sustaining goods. However, she erroneously assumed that individuals consume life-sustaining goods only if they produce life-sustaining goods. It is not necessary that the one who consumes life-sustaining goods must also produce. He could be given them by others who produce. Second, Smith implied that restricting freedom of action results in a corresponding threat to life. But that inference does not follow. Individuals could produce more than they need – not merely for the sake of luxury and security, but also for the sake of others whom they care for or for the sake of duty without ever experiencing a threat to life. Therefore, it is ironic, and certainly contrary to common expectations, that a set of rights grounded in economic efficiency appears to be less individualistic and more communitarian than Smith's rights, which are based on her view of the person.

33 My discussion is significantly influenced by Morris (1976) and by conversations with Ronald Koshoshek.

34 What I describe is what Ullmann-Margalit (1977) calls an 'inequality-preserving institution."

35 Compare Sen (1970b: 87).

36 Intentional externalities are precluded when each individual observes the substan-

tive rights. Observing others' right to welfare requires that a set of procedures for rectifying the relevant types of results of accidental externalites are in place.

37 However, the system specified in this book could be supplemented in various ways with other rights and procedures thereby serving as the common core of several different systems. Being compatible with a range of alternative moral perspectives is a philosophical and practical desideratum.

7. Implications

1 On the concept of the market compare recent literature: Bonner (1986), Fourie (1993), Hodgson (1988), Moss (1981,1984), and Sawyer (1993). Geoffrey Hodgson (1988: 172) wrote,

> Mathematical models of market phenomena abound, and there is a voluminous literature on the theoretical determinants of market equilibria. Yet if we ask the elementary question – "What is a market"? – we are given short shrift. . . . Unfortunately, economists have not only shown a general negligence in defining the market, but also have been extremely cavalier in their use of the term. Thus, for example, in his analysis of marriage Gary Becker (1976, p. 206) states without hesitation that "a *market* in marriages can be presumed to exist" [emphasis in original]. Clearly, institutions such as marriage bureaux do exist. However, these are not markets (or at least not markets for marriages *per se*).

2 See Coval and Smith (1986). Since mechanism design theory focuses on information and incentive compatible rules, it cannot provide solutions to such accidental externalities.

3 "Individual factor endowments" indicates that each agents possess some ability to produce. "Private goods" indicates that each commodity enters into the utility function of only one person. "Mutual unconcern" indicates that individuals are selfish.

4 Whether selling oneself on the basis of maximizing utility avoids the problems mentioned here is an issue for another day.

Bibliography

Arrow, Kenneth J. (1969) [1992]. "The Organization of Economic Activity: Issues Pertinent to the Choice of Market Versus Non-market Allocation," in John Martin Gilroy and Maurice Wade (eds.), *The Moral Dimensions of Public Policy Choice*. Pittsburgh: University of Pittsburgh Press.

Axelrod, Robert (1984). *The Evolution of Cooperation*. New York: Basic Books.

Baumol, William J., and Alan S. Blinder (1991). *Microeconomics: Principles and Policy*. San Diego: Harcourt Brace Jovanovich.

Becker, Gary (1976). *The Economic Approach to Human Behavior*. Chicago: University of Chicago Press.

Becker, Lawrence (1977). *Property Rights: Philosophic Foundations*. London: Routledge & Kegan Paul.

   (1980). "The Moral Basis of Property Rights," in J Roland Pinnock and John W. Chapman (eds.), *Property: NOMOS XXII*. New York: New York University.

Beckman, F. S. (1980). *Mathematical Foundations of Programming*. Reading, Mass.: Addison-Wesley.

Binmore, Ken (1994). *Game Theory and the Social Contract: Volume 1, Playing Fair*. Cambridge, Mass.: The MIT Press.

Bonner, John (1986). *Introduction to the Theory of Social Choice*. Baltimore: Johns Hopkins University Press.

Boolos, George S., and Richard C. Jeffrey (1989). *Computability and Logic*. Cambridge: Cambridge University Press.

Bourdieu, Pierre (1990). *The Logic of Practice*. Stanford: Stanford University Press.

Buchanan, James M. (1989). *Explorations into Constitutional Economics*. College Station: Texas A&M University Press.

Bush, Winston C., and Lawrence S. Mayer (1974). "Some implications of Anarchy for the Distribution of Property," *Journal of Economic Theory* 8: 401–12.

Calabresi, Guido, and A. Douglas Melamed (1972). "Property Rules, Liability Rules, and inalienability: One View of the Cathedral," *Harvard Law Review* 85: 1089–128.

Coase, R. H. (1960). "The Problem of Social Cost," *The Journal of Law and Economics* 3: 1–44.

Coleman, James (1990). *Foundations of Social Theory*. Cambridge, Mass.: Harvard University Press.

Coleman, Jules (1992). *Risks and Wrongs.* Cambridge: Cambridge University Press.

 (1988 [1985]). "Market Contractarianism," in Jules A. Coleman (ed.), *Markets, Morals, and the Law.* Cambridge: Cambridge University Press.

Coleman, Jules, and Jodie Kraus (1988), "Rethinking the Theory of Legal Rights," in Jules A. Coleman (ed.), *Markets, Morals, and the Law.* Cambridge: Cambridge University Press.

Cooter, Robert, and Thomas Ulen (1997). *Law and Economics,* Reading, Mass.: Addison Wesley.

Copp, David, (1995). *Morality, Normativity, and Society.* Oxford: Oxford University Press.

Coval, S. C., and J. C. Smith (1986). *Law and Its Presuppositions.* London: Rutledge & Kegan Paul.

Davis, John (1992). *Exchange.* Minneapolis: University of Minnesota Press.

Davis, Martin (1973). *Computability and Unsolvability.* New York: Dover Publications.

Evensky, Jerry (1993). "Ethics and the Invisible Hand," *Journal of Economic Perspectives* (17) 2: 197–205.

Feinberg, Joel (1970 [1979]). "The Nature and Value of Rights," in David Lyons (ed.), *Rights.* Belmont, Calif.: Wadsworth Publishing Company.

Ferguson, Adam (1767 [1966]). D. Forbes (ed.), *An Essay on the History of Civil Society.* Edinburgh: University Press.

Field, Alexander James (1984). "Microeconomics, Norms and Rationality," *Economic Development and Cultural Change* 32: 683–711.

Flanagan, Owen (1991). *Varieties of Moral Personality: Ethics and Psychological Realism.* Cambridge, Mass.: Harvard University Press.

Fourie, Frederick C. v. N. (1993). "In the Beginning There Were Markets," in Christos Pitelis (ed.), *Transaction Costs, Markets and Hierarchies,* pp. 41–65. Cambridge, Mass: Basil Blackwell.

Frey, Bruno (1992). *Economics as a Science of Human Behavior: Towards a New Social Science Paradigm.* Boston: Kluwer Academic Publishers.

Friedman, Milton, and Rose Friedman (1980). *Free to Choose: A Personal Statement.* New York: Harcourt Brace Jovanovich.

Gaertner, Wulf, Prasanta K. Pattanaik, and Kotaro Suzumara (1992). "Individual Rights Revisited," *Economica* 59: 161–77.

Gauthier, David (1982). "No Need for Morality: The Case of the Competitive Market," *Philosophic Exchange* 3 (3): 41–54.

 (1986). *Morals by Agreement.* Oxford: Clarendon Press.

Gewirth, Alan, (1978). *Reason and Morality.* Chicago: The University of Chicago Press.

 (1993) "Common Morality and the Community of Rights," in *Prospects for a Common Morality.* Princeton: Princeton University Press.

Gilbert, Margaret (1989). *On Social Facts.* Princeton: Princeton University Press.

Greenberg, Joseph (1990). *The Theory of Social Situations: An Alternative Game-Theoretic Approach.* Cambridge: Cambridge University Press.

Hampton, Jean (1988). "Forgiveness, Resentment and Hatred," in *Forgiveness and Mercy,* Cambridge: Cambridge University Press.

 (1997). *Political Philosophy.* Boulder, Colo.: Westview.

Hardin, Russell (1982). *Collective Action.* Baltimore: Johns Hopkins University Press.

 (1988). *Morality Within the Limits of Reason.* Chicago: University of Chicago Press.

Hart, H. L. A. (1994 [1961]). *The Concept of Law,* 2nd ed. Oxford: Clarendon Press.

Haslett, D. W. (1994). *Capitalism with Morality.* Oxford: Clarendon Press.

Hayek, F. A. (1960). *The Constitution of Liberty.* Chicago: University of Chicago Press.

(1964). "Kinds of Order in Society." *New Individualist Review* 2 (3): 3–12.

Heap, Shaun P. Hargreaves, and Yanis Varoufakis (1995). *Game Theory: A Critical Introduction.* London and New York: Routledge.

Hirshleifer, Jack (1985). "The Expanding Domain of Economics," *American Economic Review* 6: 53–68.

Hodgson, Geoffrey M. (1988). *Economics and Institutions: A Manifesto for Modern Institutional Economics.* Cambridge: Polity Press; Philadelphia: University of Pennsylvania Press.

Hohfeld, Wesley Newcomb (1919 [1978]). *Fundamental Legal Conceptions as Applied in Judicial Reasoning,* Walter W. Cook (ed.) Westport, Conn.: Greenwood Press.

Honoré, A. M. (1961). "Ownership," in A. G. Guest (ed.), *Oxford Essays in Jurisprudence (First Series),* pp. 107–47. Oxford: Clarendon Press.

Hume, David (1739 [1975]). *A Treatise of Human Nature,* L. A. Selby-Bigge (ed.) Oxford: The Clarendon Press.

Hurwicz, Leonid (1972). "On Informationally Decentralized Systems," in R. Radner and C. B. McGuires (eds.), *Decision and Organization: A Volume in Honor of Jacob Marshak,* pp. 297–336. Amsterdam: North-Holland.

(1973). "The Design of Mechanisms for Resource Allocation," *American Economic Review* 63 (2): 1–30.

(1993). "Implementation and Enforcement in Institutional Modeling," in W. A. Barnett, M. J. Hinich, and N. J. Schofield (eds.), *Political Economy: Institutions, Competition and Representation,* chapter 2. Cambridge: Cambridge University Press.

(1996). "Institutions as Families of Game Forms," in *The Japanese Economic Review* 47 (2): 113–32.

Karni, Edi (1989). "Fraud," in John Eatwell, Murray Milgate, and Peter Newman (eds.), *The New Palgrave: Allocation, Information, and Markets.* London: W. W. Norton.

Koopmans, Tjalling Charles (1957). *Three Essays on the State of Economic Science.* New York: McGraw Hill.

Kuflik, Arthur (1992). "The Inalienability of Autonomy," in John Martin Gilroy and Maurice Wade (eds.), *The Moral Dimensions of Public Policy Choice: Beyond the Market Paradigm,* pp. 465–89. Pittsburgh, Penn.: University of Pittsburgh Press.

Lewis, David (1969). *Convention: A Philosophical Study.* Cambridge, Mass.: Harvard University Press.

Lomasky, Loren E. (1987). *Persons, Rights, and the Moral Community.* Oxford: Oxford University Press.

Macleod, Alistair (1996). *Invisible Hand Arguments and the Free Market Ideal,* working paper delivered at the Central Division Meeting of the American Philosophical Association Chicago, Ill., April 1996.

Malitz, Jerome (1979). *Introduction to Mathematical Logic: Set Theory, Computable Functions, Model Theory.* New York: Springer-Verlag.

Margolis, Howard (1982). *Selfishness, Rationality, and Altruism: A Theory of Social Choice.* Chicago: University of Chicago Press.

(1984). *Patterns, Thinking and Cognition.* Chicago: University of Chicago Press.

(1990). "Dual Utilities and Rational Choice," in Karen Schweers Cook and Margaret Levi (eds.), *The Limits of Rationality,* pp. 239–53. Chicago: University of Chicago Press.

Martin, Rex (1993). *A System of Rights.* Oxford: Clarendon Press.

Mas-Colell, Andreu, Michael D. Whinston, and Jerry R. Green (1995). *Microeconomic Theory.* Oxford: Oxford University Press.

Matthews, R. C. O. (1981). "Morality, Competition and Efficiency," *Manchester School of Economic and Social Studies* 49 (4): 289–309.

Menger, Carl (1981 [1871]). *Principles of Economics.* New York: New York University Press.

    (1985 [1883]). *Investigations into the Method of the Social Sciences with Special Reference to Economics.* New York and London: New York University Press.

Morris, Herbert (1976). "Persons and Punishment," *On Guilt and Innocence: Essays in Legal Philosophy and Moral Psychology.* Berkeley: University of California Press.

Moss, Scott J. (1981). *An Economic Theory of Business Strategy: An Essay in Dynamics without Equilibrium.* Oxford: Martin Robertson.

    (1984). *Markets and Macroeconomics: Macroeconomic Implications of Rational Economic Behavior.* Oxford: Basil Blackwell.

Munzer, Stephen R. (1990). *A Theory of Property.* Cambridge: Cambridge University Press.

Myerson, Roger B. (1989). "Mechanism Design," in John Eatwell, Murray Milgate, and Peter Newman (eds.), *The New Palgrave: Allocation, Information, and Markets,* pp. 191–206. London: W. W. Norton.

Nida-Rümelin, Julian (1991). "Practical Reason or Metapreferences? An Undogmatic Defense of Kantian Morality," *Theory and Decision* 30: 133–62.

North, Douglass (1990). "Institutions and Their Consequences for Economic Preference," in Karen Schweers Cook and Margaret Levi (eds.), *The Limits of Rationality,* pp. 383–401. Chicago: The University of Chicago Press.

Nozick, Robert (1974). *Anarchy, State, and Utopia.* New York: Basic Books.

Oliner, Samuel, and Pearl Oliner (1988). *The Altruistic Personality: Rescuers of Jews in Nazi Europe.* New York: Free Press.

Ostrom, Elinor, Roy Gardner, and James Walker (1994) *Rules, Games, and Common-Pool Resources.* Ann Arbor: University of Michigan Press.

Papandreou, Andreas (1994). *Externality and Institutions.* Oxford: Oxford University Press.

Pettit, Philip (1990). "*Virtus Normativa:* Rational Choice Perspectives," *Ethics* 100: 725–55.

Posner, Richard (1992). *The Economics Analysis of Law.* Boston: Little, Brown.

Postema, Gerald (1982). "Coordination and Convention at the Foundations of Law," *Journal of Legal Studies* 11: 165–203.

Rawls, John (1971). *A Theory of Justice.* Cambridge, Mass.: The Bellknap Press of Harvard University Press.

    (1993). *Political Liberalism.* New York: Columbia University Press.

Raz, Joseph (1990). *Practical Reason and Norms.* Princeton: Princeton University Press.

Reynolds, Noel B. (1989). "Law as Convention," *Ratio Juris* 2(1): 105–20.

Sawyer, Malcolm C. (1993). "The Nature and Role of the Market," in Christos Pitelis (ed.), *Transaction Costs, Markets and Hierarchies,* pp. 20–40. Cambridge, Mass.: Basil Blackwell.

Schmidtz, David (1995). *Rational Choice and Moral Agency.* Princeton: Princeton University Press.

Schotter, Andrew (1981). *The Economic Theory of Social Institutions.* Cambridge: Cambridge University Press.

Searle, John (1995). *The Construction of Social Reality.* New York: Free Press.

Sen, Amartya (1970a). "The Impossibility of a Paretian Liberal," *Journal of Political Economy,* 78: 152–7.

(1970b). *Collective Choice and Social Welfare.* San Francisco: Holden-day.

(1977). "Rational Fools: A Critique of the Behavioral Foundations of Economic Theory," *Philosophy and Public Affairs,* 6: 316–44.

(1980). "Description as Choice," *Oxford Economic Papers,* 32: 353–69.

(1992). "Minimal Liberty," *Economica* 59: 139–59.

Smiley, Marion (1992). *Moral Responsibility and the Boundaries of Community.* Chicago: University of Chicago Press.

Smith, Adam (1759 [1976]). *A Theory of Moral Sentiments,* D. D. Raphael and A. L. Macfie (eds.). London: Oxford University Press.

(1763 [1978]). *Lectures on Jurisprudence,* R. L. Meek, D. D. Raphael, and P. G. Stein (eds.). Oxford: Oxford University Press.

(1776 [1976]). *An Inquiry into the Nature and Causes of the Wealth of Nations,* R. H. Campbell, A. S. Skinner, and W. B. Todd (eds.). London: Oxford University Press.

(1795 [1980]). *Essays on Philosophical Subjects.* Oxford: Oxford University Press.

Smith, Tara (1995). *Moral Rights and Political Freedom.* Lanham, Md.: Rowman & Littlefield Publishers.

Steiner, Hillel (1994). *An Essay on Rights.* Oxford: Blackwell.

Sugden, Robert (1989). "Spontaneous-Order," *Journal of Economic Perspectives,* 4(3): 85–97.

(1994). "The Theory of Rights," in Horst Siebert (ed.), *The Ethical Foundations of the Market Economy: International Workshop.* Tübingen: J. C. B. Mohe (Paul Siebeck).

Taylor, Michael (1990). "Cooperation and Rationality: Notes on the Collective Action Problem and Its Solutions," in Karen Schweers Cook and Margaret Levi (eds.), *The Limits of Rationality,* pp. 222–40. Chicago: University of Chicago Press.

Thomson, Judith Jarvis (1990). *The Realm of Rights.* Cambridge, Mass.: Harvard University Press.

Trebilcock, Michael J. (1993). *The Limits of Freedom of Contract.* Cambridge, Mass.: Harvard University Press.

Turing, Alan (1936). "On Computable Numbers, with an Application to the Entscheidungsproblem," *Proceedings of the London Mathematical Society,* Ser. 2, 42: 230–65; 43: 544–6.

Ullmann-Margalit, Edna (1977). *The Emergence of Norms.* Oxford: Oxford University Press.

Usher, Dan (1992). *The Welfare Economics of Markets, Voting, and Predation.* Ann Arbor: The University of Michigan Press.

Vanberg, Viktor (1994). *Rules and Choice in Economics.* London: Routledge.

van Hees, Martin (1995). *Rights and Decisions.* Dordrecht: Kluwer Academic Publishers.

Varian, Hal R. (1992). *Microeconomic Analysis.* New York: W. W. Norton.

Walras, Leon (1874). *Elements of Pure Economics,* W. Jaffé, ed. and trans. London: Allen & Unwin.

Wellman, Carl (1982). *Welfare Rights.* Totowa, N.J.: Rowman & Allanheld.

(1985). *A Theory of Rights: Persons Under Laws, Institutions, and Morals.* Totowa, N.J.: Rowman & Allanheld.

(1995). *Real Rights.* Oxford: Oxford University Press.

Yasuhara, Ann (1971). *Recursive Function Theory and Logic.* New York: Academic Press.

Index